Moulton College

NORTHAMPTONSHIRE

Profit through Skill

Improving People Performance in Construction

IMPROVING PEOPLE PERFORMANCE IN CONSTRUCTION

David Cooper

GOWER

Published by
Gower Publishing Limited
Gower House
Croft Road
Aldershot
Hants GU11 3HR
England

Gower Publishing Company
Suite 420
101 Cherry Street
Burlington
VT 05401-4405
USA

British Library Cataloguing in Publication Data
Cooper, David J. (David John), 1950–
   Improving people performance in construction. – (The
   leading construction series)
   1. Construction industry – Management 2. Construction
   industry – Personnel management 3. Employee motivation
   4. Leadership
   I. Title
   624'.0684

   ISBN 0 566 08617 4

Library of Congress Cataloging-in-Publication Data
Cooper, David.
   Improving people performance in construction / by David Cooper.
      p. cm. -- The leading construction series
   Includes index
   ISBN: 0-566-08617-4
   1. Construction industry -- Management. 2. Construction industry -- Personnel management
   3. Construction industry -- Employees -- Training of. I. Title. II. Series.
   HD9715.A2C658 2004
   624'.068'3--dc22

                                                                              2004010519

Typeset by Secret Genius, 11 Mons Court, Winchester SO23 8GH.
Printed in Great Britain by MPG Books Ltd, Bodmin, Cornwall.

Contents

List of Figures   vii
List of Tables   ix
List of Self-assessment Charts and Questionnaires   xi
List of Abbreviations   xiii
Introduction   xv

Chapter 1 – The Construction Industry: The Context
Introducing the context   2
The changing environment   2
Government initiatives for change   3
Health and safety   5
Performance management   7
Competence   9
The knowledge economy   17
Summary   18

Chapter 2 – Improving People Performance: The Approach
Managers and leaders   20
Leadership in the workplace   22
Management and leadership style   24
Employee commitment: what does it look like?   30
Motivation   32
Employee satisfaction   36
Rewards and incentives   42
Summary   49
Conclusion   49

Chapter 3 – Performance Management Strategies
Company objectives and strategic plans   53
Communication: What a manager needs to know   57
Asking questions and giving feedback   69
Recruiting and selecting people   72
How to introduce people to the company   80
The manager as teambuilder and team leader   82
The manager's toolbox of skills   86
Retaining people   98
Summary   102

Chapter 4 – Performance Management Methods
Introduction   104
Performance agreements and setting objectives   105
Performance measures/indicators (KPIs)   107
Benchmarking   114
Individual behavioural performance   117
The manager as appraiser   118
Training and developing your people and your personal development   127
Investors in People (IiP)   134
Dealing with performance problems   136
Summary   141

Chapter 5 – Future Strategies?
Lessons for managers: pulling it all together   144
The Balanced Scorecard   147
The EFQM Excellence Model™   151
The learning company   154
A manager's prayer   156

References and Further Reading   157
Useful Addresses   161
Index   163

List of Figures

2.1	*A different way of thinking?*	25
2.2	*From motivation to level of job performance*	34
2.3	*Herzberg's motivators and hygiene factors*	37
2.4	*Forms of recognition*	47
3.1	*Extract from a draft company mission statement*	55
3.2	*Sample job specification form*	74
3.3	*Sample person specification form*	75
4.1	*Sample monthly and annual summary of absence form*	113
4.2	*Sample personal development record*	120
4.3	*Sample performance management personal preparation form*	123
4.4	*Sample performance management manager's preparation form*	124
4.5	*Sample performance management review record form*	125
4.6	*Sample learning contract*	128
4.7	*Using training, coaching and counselling skills to deal with performance problems*	138
5.1	*The Balanced Scorecard – strategic objectives*	148
5.2	*The EFQM Excellence Model™*	152

List of Tables

1.1   *Injuries to employees in the construction sector reported to all enforcement authorities (2000–2002)*   6

1.2   *Kinds of accident to employees in the construction sector reported to the HSE's Field Operations Division Inspectorates and local authorities during 2001–2002*   6

2.1   *Characteristics of managers and leaders according to Bennis*   20

2.2   *Activities of managers and leaders according to Kotter*   20

2.3   *'Good' leadership characteristics: the directors' view*   28

2.4   *Leadership behaviours and attitudes that encourage high performance from people* 29

2.5   *People's needs*   35

2.6   *Motivation: workers' and managers' perspectives (Couger and Zawacki)*   46

2.7   *Motivation: workers' and managers' perspectives (Kovach)*   47

3.1   *Typical policies and procedures relating to people and performance management*   56

3.2   *Improvements attributed to communication initiatives*   58

4.1   *The ten construction industry KPIs*   109

4.2   *Summary of industry performance – 'Respect for People' KPIs – 2001*   112

List of Self-assessment Charts and Questionnaires

Self-assessment questionnaire: competencies   11

Self-assessment chart: competency ratings   16

Self-assessment questionnaire: communication skills   60

Stress assessment chart   62

BSC	balanced scorecard
BSc	Bachelor of Science
CBI	Confederation of British Industry
CEO	chief executive officer
CITB	Construction Industry Training Board
DTI	Department of Trade and Industry
ECS	Employee Commitment Survey
EFQM	European Foundation for Quality Management
GNVQ	General National Vocational Qualification
GSS	General Satisfaction Survey
HNC	Higher National Certificate
HND	Higher National Diploma
HR	human resources
HRM	human resource management
HRS	human resource strategy
HSE	Health and Safety Executive
IiP	Investors in People
KPI	key performance indicator
M4I	Movement for Innovation
MBA	Masters in Business Administration
MD	managing director
MSc	Master of Science
NVQ	National Vocational Qualification
PPI	people performance indicator
PRP	performance-related pay
SMART	Stretching, Measurable, Agreed, Realistic and Relevant, Time-bounded
SME	small- to medium-sized enterprise

This book is written for managers in the construction industry as a practical guide towards improving people performance. It uses the backdrop provided by the banner of Sir John Egan's Construction Task Force's *Rethinking Construction* (Egan, 1998) report which maintains that people are our industry's biggest asset.

It is people like you and me that make the difference between poor and highly effective company performance. We do this by being willing to apply our knowledge, skills and commitment towards the achievement of company objectives. As managers, however, we are also directly responsible for others doing the same. This is an important role for managers because it is the sum of individual performances of people, whatever their grade or work role, that leads to better company performance, competitive advantage and continued employment.

So, how can you work towards ensuring that your organization performs well? Clearly, you need the right people in the right place at the right time with the right knowledge, skills and willingness – not easy to say and even more difficult to do. Why should you have problems? After all is said and done, more people than ever before are entering further and higher education, so exposure to relevant knowledge should not be a problem. There is also a marked upturn in vocational training, especially in skills related to the construction industry. Moreover, judging by the frustrating traffic jams on the roads in the UK, there are enough people living here, so we should not have any manpower shortages. More importantly, most people are reasonable aren't they?

Experience has taught me that getting people to perform well is very difficult. Some employees seem absolutely determined not to perform to their obvious potential. Indeed, they seem to use up much of their valuable energy making things more difficult and causing managers constant frustration. I wish I had a pound for every time a manager, regardless of level in the organization, said to me that they did not have many work problems apart from those related to the management of people. Why might this happen? Is there anything managers can do to stop, or at least contain, such problems? What do you think?

It is worth mentioning that nothing worthwhile will be simple, so it's best not to expect it. Most managers will assert that, even compared to high-technology machinery, people are complicated. They have different needs, hold differing skills and levels of knowledge, come from different backgrounds and have witnessed and/or accepted different points of view from those who have influenced them throughout their lives – for example, parents, teachers, friends, previous bosses and so on.

As a manager, it is not acceptable to simply blame employees when performance falls below tolerable levels. It is your job to improve the performance of people – however difficult. Equally, abdicating responsibility for performance and suggesting that they 'are only there to row the company boat' misses the fact that, all things being equal, gaining the commitment of people leads to high performance. This imperative should not be ignored.

I was involved in a major survey of employee satisfaction encompassing 25 000 people from shop-floor to managing director level. The most significant issue arising from the survey was that many employees reported a lack of commitment. It was my job to uncover the underlying causes. My investigation indicated the need for more effective people management and process – for example, effective recruitment, retention, training, development, personnel procedures and so on. What's more, I found that the ability of managers to use people management skills was important to enabling employees to develop enthusiasm and work effectively. Consequently, to improve people performance we need to review and address people-related systems, process and behaviour.

The approach of this book acknowledges that most people under the right organizational and managerial conditions can – and will – perform well. They achieve good performance by applying their knowledge and skills in an appropriate manner. On several occasions I have witnessed new managers take over poorly committed employees and, within a short period, all were receiving merit awards. There is something that can be learnt and applied by all managers that results in the effective management of people. Despite the difficulties, when you manage people well, the personal, individual and company rewards far outweigh any frustrations you may meet along the way.

The best way to break down the task of how to manage and improve people performance is to divide it into manageable pieces. With this in mind, the text should help you to rethink and review how people are managed in your company, assess your own management and leadership style, and adopt approaches, techniques and strategy for the continuous improvement of people performance.

To complete this introduction, I am pleased to acknowledge the valued support received from Jonathan Norman of Gower Publishing – thank you, Jonathan.

David J Cooper
2004

Chapter **1**

The Construction Industry: The Context

Introducing the context

It is tempting to race headlong into explaining effective people processes and techniques. However, as a manager, you will benefit from a general understanding of what is currently pushing the construction industry, your organization and you yourself to change. On a personal note, there is nothing worse than senior figures in your organization or your immediate boss telling you what to do without offering some reason as to why you need to do it. Consequently, this chapter aims to provide the context to why we all need to strive to improve people performance. I have chosen a few obvious themes such as the changing environment, government initiatives for change and the ongoing importance of health and safety. Also included are areas that set the scene for the whole book – performance management, competence and the knowledge economy.

The changing environment

The need for change urges managers to make internal adjustments that pressure the workforce to respond. The response we require is for employees to improve their performance and increase the value of their work. However, we may all react differently to change in our lives. For example, you may view change as stressful, or you may see it as a challenge and as a means to overcome the normal day-to-day boredom of working life. In the past, managers tended to see change as a response to a specific problem. Perhaps you view change as something that you go all out to subdue in order to have a quiet life and be able to work within a stable working environment.

'... managers will need to gain the willing contribution of a diverse workforce in order to target new markets and distinguish their products and services from the competition.' (Worman, 1996)

Regardless of your view of change, to improve performance we need to accept that change is generic, constant, all around us, and for most organizations it provides a 'white water' context. More importantly, change is something you need to understand or even instigate in order to improve performance and aid competitive advantage. This is true for all sectors: business, government, healthcare, social, non-profit and so on.

Change is something you need to instigate.

Companies in the construction industry need to produce goods and services in a fast, consistent, flexible and responsive way that reflects value for money and gains customer satisfaction. Firms that cannot adopt such an approach are unlikely to benefit from changing market conditions. We also need effective management and leadership that encourage employees to follow willingly. We need a workforce that is not only empowered, but well managed, encouraged and rewarded.

Grim (2001) comments that the way we think also needs to change from metres/sec to metres/sec^2. From experience, I am not sure I totally agree that the increasing speed of change is always fun

– that being pushed back into your seat with your eyeballs pressing back on the brain is always exhilarating. Nevertheless, I do agree that in order to survive and thrive you may need to change the way you think about change and adopt skills and techniques that get the best out of your staff/workforce.

There are plenty of traditional ways of working in the construction industry and you need to revisit and perhaps review these to check they are providing you with the support you need to improve performance. A few old managerial practices and approaches will have to go and be replaced with far more professional behaviour and the use of appropriate processes and techniques.

I will try not to sound too academic; however, a further quote from Grim seems to capture the 'new-born' management philosophy – 'It's the people that make the difference, stupid.' People issues may take up most of your time and present you with what sometimes feel like unsolvable problems, but they are also the very foundation of your organization – whatever its size.

Government initiatives for change

The UK construction industry provides a tenth of the UK's gross domestic product and employs approximately 1.5 million people. It employs designers, civil engineers, contractors and component and product manufacturers, of which approximately 600 000 are self-employed. Typical job titles include technicians, carpenters, joiners, plumbers, plasterers, painters, glazers, roofers, floorers, scaffolders, plant operatives, other civil engineers and, of course, managers who might or might not have a professional title and/or qualification. According to the 2002 Labour Force Survey, the industry is male-dominated with an approximate ratio of 9:1 and is one of the strongest in the world, with output ranked in the global top ten. However, it wants to improve its standing. Consequently, if we are interested in why change is occurring, understanding top-down Government schemes and initiatives is a vital starting point.

The Department of Trade and Industry (DTI) introduced the topic of *Rethinking Construction*, a major industry-led initiative to improve the performance of the construction industry. Initiated by the report of the construction task force chaired by Sir John Egan in 1998, important principles were offered:

1 the need for client leadership
2 the need for integrated teams through the delivery chain
3 the need for a respect for people.

Targets for improvement that underpin *Rethinking Construction* and provide for local as well as national measures of improvement are:

1 reduced capital cost
2 reduced construction time
3 better predictability
4 fewer defects
5 fewer accidents
6 increased productivity
7 increased turnover (sales) and profit.

Various influential reports have provided an additional backdrop urging improvement. For example, *Accelerating Change* (Strategic Forum, 2002) reported progress since *Rethinking Construction* – four years on. It commented that the *Rethinking Construction* objectives were, and still are, to achieve radical improvements in the design, quality, sustainability and customer satisfaction of UK construction. However, some important areas still need to be addressed within the *Rethinking Construction* agenda. These are as follows:

1 Continue to prove the business case for change through demonstrations, with a growing emphasis on organization change projects.
2 Identify gaps in the business case that need to be filled.
3 Take the message to small- to medium-sized enterprises (SMEs) and encourage their wider involvement.
4 Build a strong national support network across all the English regions, Northern Ireland, Scotland and Wales.

Based on progress, the DTI gave the *Rethinking Construction* initiative its continued financial support. The initiative is also backed through the direct involvement of hundreds of companies and government departments including the Treasury and the Department of Transport, local government and the regions, as well as the Housing Corporation.

Perhaps more closely related to people performance, the report, *Respect for People – A 'Framework for Action'*, was written by the Respect for People Working Group (2003a) as a key element of the *Rethinking Construction* agenda. It offers recommendations such as:

- All organizations should consider the appointment of champions to support operational managers in improving people performance.
- Every firm should appoint someone at board level to take overall responsibility for people issues and to regularly monitor and evaluate performance.
- Every company and project should adequately address and provide quantifiable data on 'people' issues.
- A simple client guide to best practice in covering *Respect for People* in construction should be developed.

*How well does your
company perform
against these targets?*

- Toolkits (measuring and aiding review of key performance indicators or KPIs) should be trialled.
- The underpinning data relating to people performance should be standardized and collected at least annually across the construction sector.
- There should be better coordination among key partners to monitor and review progress towards the industry *Respect for People* targets to ensure they are delivered.
- The business case for training should be developed further.
- The number of construction workers working for firms recognized as an 'Investor in People' should increase by 20 per cent per annum.
- The industry should substantially increase the number of people entering it from underrepresented groups with an initial target of not less than 20 per cent per annum.
- The industry should wholly adopt the *Rethinking Construction* target of a 20 per cent per annum reduction in reportable incidents.
- All employers and project teams should measure – at least annually – their whole workforce to determine their satisfaction with working conditions and environment.

The key theme of *A Commitment to People – 'Our Biggest Asset'* (Respect for People, 2003b) strongly suggests the need to have a respect for people. It also suggests a strong business case for improvements hinged on the three Rs. Firms failing to 'Respect' people will fail to 'Recruit' and 'Retain' them. *Reaching the Standard (Respect for People,* 2002) offered key information about toolkits and benchmarking (explained in Chapter 4) and made important linkages with Investors in People, ISO 9000–2000 and the European Foundation for Quality Management, (EFQM) – Excellence Model™. You will find an interpretation of links with this model in Chapter 5.

Health and safety

Regardless of the industry, market, company, country or region, health and safety must be an area for your concern when considering the working environment and people performance. People cannot perform if they are injured. Clearly, we all have an obligation to make sure that colleagues work in the most safe and healthy environment possible. It is obvious to most that some industries are at greater risk than others when it comes to ensuring the health and safety of people – that is, employees, customers and users. Just because you work in construction does not mean that risk and accidents are inevitable. However, the figures speak for themselves (see Tables 1.1 and 1.2).

Category	Total*
Fatal injuries	85
Non-fatal major injuries	4862
Injuries lasting over 3 days	9587

* Employees, self-employed and members of the public.

Source: DTI (2002).

Table 1.1 *Injuries to employees in the construction sector reported to all enforcement authorities (2001–2002)*

Accident	Total
Contact with moving machinery	384
Struck by moving/flying object	2154
Struck by moving vehicle	234
Strike against something fixed or stationary	529
Injured whilst handling, lifting or carrying	3503
Slip, trip or fall on same level	2986
Fall from a height	2174
Trapped by something collapsing or overturning	72
Exposure to or contact with a harmful substance	285
Exposure to fire	44
Exposure to explosion	22
Contact with electricity or an electrical discharge	129
Acts of violence	68

Source: DTI (2002).

Table 1.2 *Kinds of accident to employees in the construction sector reported to the HSE's Field Operations Division Inspectorates and local authorities during 2001–2002*

HSE enforcement notices, served in the construction industry to stop work until an imminent risk of personal injury is eliminated, totalled 2745 in the year 2001–02, a rise of 27 per cent compared with 1993–94. Proceedings taken by the HSE's field operations inspectorates in the same year resulted in 431 convictions and an average fine per conviction of £7594. For further statistics you may wish to get in touch with the DTI to review their annually released figures.

There has been a 27 per cent increase in HSE enforcement notices in the construction industry since 1993.

Health and safety remains a key consideration for the construction industry. The Department of Trade and Industry comments that: 'It is one of the key issues that impair the public's perception of the industry' – and, I might add, perhaps the perception of potential future employees. A wide-ranging discussion document, *Revitalising Health and Safety in Construction* (HSE, 2002) has been launched. This document reviews the current state of the industry and notes that performance in health and safety cannot be separated from performance in other key business areas – for example, quality, timely delivery and profitability. *Respect for People: A Framework for Action* asserts that too little conscious attention is also given to occupational ill-health: 'By its nature, ill-health effects are usually slow to be realized, but its costs and long-term implications are far more significant than those of accidents where there are immediate visible impacts.' Clearly, the working environment and safe working conditions are important to employee motivation. The issue of motivation is considered in Chapter 2.

Safe working conditions are important to the motivation of your employees.

Performance management

Performance management is all about how performance can be improved and developed.

The idea of managing people performance arose in the late 1980s. It grew in importance because everyone realized that managers needed a continuous and flexible approach to their workforce that sets out how to work together to improve performance. Performance management has some distinct features:

1   It is a process that accepts that your performance (and your staff/employees' performance) can be developed and improved.
2   It is based on both individual and team performance.
3   It is a process that measures and reviews how you and your staff/employees perform.
4   It is concerned with your skills, knowledge, and behaviour – your competencies, and the competencies of your staff/employees.

Everything in this book relates and builds on those aspects of performance management. Chapters 3 and 4 explain in detail the strategies and techniques associated with performance management, such as how to put plans together, how to set, measure and review performance objectives, the role of training and development, dealing with performance problems and so on. Step-by-step guidelines are provided.

Of course, you need to use performance-related techniques instinctively and effectively. At the core of performance lies the manager–employee relationship – a relationship that is likely to have been built up over many years. Its roots may be historic and involve different people.

You will be aware of how you feel about the people who report to you. You will have views about their skills, knowledge, attitudes and behaviour. Perhaps you hold some good impressions and some not so good; nevertheless, what you think of your employees will affect the way you manage them. In the same way, your colleagues, your own manager and your staff will hold opinions about you. For instance, your manager's view about how effective you are in your job will probably affect your career, your colleagues' opinions will affect the way they communicate with you, and your people will have a view about you which affects their everyday performance on the job. Your people's perception of you as their manager is critical – would you work harder for a boss you did not respect?

It is possible that many frustrations experienced by your staff are beyond your control, and you simply receive the backlash from issues that you see arising from decisions made by your superiors. But if you are seeking improved performance you will be interested in your people's perception. Consequently, all blockages to performance are in some way the responsibility of every manager – avoiding some responsibility is inappropriate, even if your response is only a matter of ensuring more senior managers understand the issues affecting your people's performance. In some cases, people may be willing to tell you face-to-face what they think of you and what they think of your ability to manage them – perhaps using some quite colourful language along the way. I far prefer staff who are willing to let me know what it is that may be preventing them from performing better, even if 'choice' words are sometimes used and even if part (or all) of the problem is me.

From experience, I have found that if an employee holds a favourable perception of you as their manager the more likely they are to perform well in their job. However, I must stress that I am definitely not suggesting that managers should spend their days going 'all-out' to please each and every one of their staff, all the time. That would be naive and impossible. And, even if it were possible, the cost of doing so would be prohibitive to the organization. Quite simply, you cannot please everyone all of the time. Chapters 2 and 3 will help clarify what good efficient management and effective leadership of people and teams really looks like. For now, let me simply report a conversation held with someone I respect, who is an exceptional manager of people. The conversation took place immediately following his retirement. I asked him, 'What things do you wish you had been told when you first became a manager?' He responded:

A manager is responsible for making sure people do the right jobs in the right way at the right time.

- 'Being a manager is different from being a colleague. You can't be one of the lads (or lasses) and a manager at the same time. You can't easily manage your best mate.'
- 'The difference between a supervisor and a manager is that a supervisor is mainly concerned with making sure that people "do the job right". A manager is also responsible for making sure people do the right jobs.'
- 'As a manager you are part of the team you lead but you are totally responsible for it, so it has to be clear that there is a difference between you and the rest of the team. Ultimately, you are the one with overall accountability and authority.'

- 'If someone badly criticizes my people, I have found that the best thing to do is defend them but investigate the matter later. Nobody has the right to have a go at my team, except me. I don't care what they have done! I'll defend them first and sort it out with them later.'

'But at my back I always hear Time's winged chariot hurrying near.' Andrew Marvell (1621–1678).

- 'Time management is crucial, but there's never enough time – so you have to be as good as you can at making the most of it. Remember, everyone else has the same problem – so don't waste other people's time.'
- 'You have to learn how to translate high-level objectives into blocks of work for your team. Expect lots of conflicting issues that you will have to resolve.'
- 'Delegating is one of the most difficult things for a manager to do well – it's about the 'how' more than the 'what'. It requires a lot of trust and you must learn not to keep checking up between normal progress meetings.'
- 'As a manager, you will at some time be responsible for recruiting people to your team. Be clear about the job you're trying to fit and the skills and experience you need the person to have. It's hard to reject people – especially if you know them personally – but do it anyway if you think they will not fit well.'
- 'As for managing money, the best advice given to me was always to think what I would do if it was my own money.'
- 'Make sure the people around you are one step ahead of the firm's need for improved levels of skill and knowledge – it's now called competency. People need to be prepared, and it's your job as manager to make sure they have the opportunity to improve.'

Competence

We say we have competent staff in surveying, architecture, engineering, project management and so on. But what exactly do we mean? Competence is a particular level of skill and knowledge. Competence is not fixed, but has many levels. Competence can range from total novice to expert, whether we are focused on bricklaying or surveying. For example, a competent architect can design – but what? An extension to a house, a factory, or a new corporate headquarters for a large multinational organization? Competence may also be seen, and perhaps measured, in terms of personal characteristics – behavioural competence. An example is the ability to lead – but lead who? One apprentice, a project team, the site workforce or an entire organization? A little more explanation may help.

The word 'competence' is often used to describe different approaches and, perhaps, different opinions about people. Competence refers to the areas of work in which a person is competent. Quite simply, they are able to demonstrate an appropriate level of competence in some or all work-related tasks. This explanation is adopted in National Vocational Qualification (NVQ) language as being a description of something that people should be able to do. Consequently, people can be assessed as to whether they can or cannot do something.

More recently, managers have been urged to see a difference between being competent and having competencies. Competencies are learned and practised skills that enable individuals to succeed in organizations. The word 'competency' suggests three important aspects. First, although many employees may be competent, some may be able to show greater competence than others – they just seem to do the job better than the average. It is up to managers to find out what makes the difference between low, average and high competence and help all workers achieve the highest competency level.

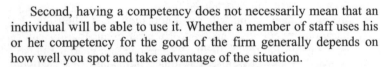

It is up to managers to find out what makes the difference between low, average and high competence.

Second, having a competency does not necessarily mean that an individual will be able to use it. Whether a member of staff uses his or her competency for the good of the firm generally depends on how well you spot and take advantage of the situation.

Finally, competency is often used to describe behaviour – for example, decisiveness, ability to take the initiative, commitment and so on. This approach might be referred to as a managerial or *behavioural* competency. It sounds complicated, but think of an employee who you know has sufficient knowledge and skills but still does not perform well. You are probably observing a person who is showing poor behavioural competency. My view is that improved performance comes about through:

1 an appropriate level of skill for each task the individual needs to perform

2 an appropriate level of knowledge about each task and how to do it

3 the individual behaving in a way that allows them to carry out the task in an efficient and effective manner

4 an environment/working climate (provided by managers) which encourages improved performance in the future via 1, 2 and 3 above.

Although construction relies heavily on craft skills, projections suggest a decline in overall numbers of skilled craftworkers. Nevertheless, in construction and specialist contracting, over half of all workers hold National Vocational Qualifications (NVQs) at level 3 or above. A quarter hold NVQ level 1 or below. A modest number hold NVQ level 4 or 5 with only 12 per cent of construction people having a degree or higher qualification. However, qualification projections by the Institute for Employment Research show an increase in the proportion of those holding levels 4 and 5 and a decline in those holding NVQ level 3 or lower.

People need skill, knowledge, commitment and support if you want them to improve.

There will also be a growing need for customer-focused staff and possibly an increase in less skilled manual workers if prefabrication techniques become more widespread. Managers will account for an increasing share of employment, and skilled crafts a declining share.

Image is important when trying to tempt new people with useful knowledge and skills into the industry. A disincentive to recruiting younger workers is the public's perception of the industry as one of hard working conditions and low pay. This means that motivational aspects, such as good training opportunities, are vital so that young employees can see the opportunity to develop and move up in the company. The Construction Industry Training Board (CITB) is leading the way in encouraging effective training programmes. This is especially important given some views that company training programmes do not entirely meet the needs of the industry. The need for appropriate training and development and for managers to develop appropriate knowledge and skill to identify, and perhaps take an active part in, training is covered in Chapter 3.

The Chartered Management Institute is clear as to vital management competency skills that relate to becoming a chartered manager. I have arranged their suggested competencies into a simple self-assessment questionnaire. Take this opportunity to rate yourself using a scale of 1 to 5. A rating of 1 would suggest that you feel you have little competence; a rating of 5 means that you feel you have already gained full competence.

Self-assessment Questionnaire: Competencies

Leading people

- I provide clear purpose and direction   [ ]
- I inspire trust, respect and shared values   [ ]
- I communicate clearly and succinctly   [ ]
- I develop and support individuals and
  team members   [ ]
- I resolve problems and conflicts with positive
  outcomes   [ ]
- I consistently apply strategic thinking   [ ]
- I adapt leadership style to take account
  of diverse situations   [ ]

Managing change

- I encourage others to be creative and
  innovative   [ ]
- I identify opportunities for change and
  development   [ ]
- I scope, plan and drive change   [ ]
- I manage others through the change process   [ ]
- I take account of all stakeholder issues   [ ]

Meeting customer needs

- I develop effective customer relationships   [ ]
- I create customer-driven improvements to
  products and services   [ ]
- I manage activities to meet customer
  requirements   [ ]
- I work to improve levels of customer
  service and satisfaction   [ ]

Managing information and knowledge

- I establish information management
  and communication systems   [ ]
- I provide and use appropriate information
  to support decision-making   [ ]
- I develop and exploit organizational
  knowledge and skills   [ ]
- I manage complexity to positive effect   [ ]

Managing activities and resources

- I optimize use of financial and other resources   [ ]
- I increase operational efficiency and
  effectiveness   [ ]
- I plan and prioritize projects and activities   [ ]
- I deliver on time, to budget and to the
  standard required   [ ]

Managing yourself

- I demonstrate resilience in achieving personal
  goals   [ ]
- I use appropriate levels of influence and
  persuasion   [ ]
- I apply good professional and ethical practice   [ ]
- I develop effective personal networks   [ ]

You may also be interested in current thinking about behavioural competencies being seen as critical to effective management performance. A friend and colleague, Trevor Mole (2003) of Property Tectonics uses the following management behavioural competencies, which he believes are suitable in today's construction and property management industry. Notice that whilst many of these focus on how people behave, they also imply a certain level of applied skill and knowledge. You might wish to judge the relevance of each competency to you and/or your specific company and working environment.

- **Adaptability**: 'The manager maintains effectiveness in stressful situations and responds positively to disappointment, rejection, frustration and setbacks.'

Comment: This competency is clearly related to personality characteristics. In a constantly changing business environment you need to remain adaptable. Your ability to manage stress is associated with your assessment of the potential stressful situation. For instance, the same situation may be seen as stressful or exciting depending on your frame of mind. Clearly, stressful situations are easier to manage if you have support from both your own manager and your firm.

- **Business awareness**: 'The manager demonstrates a sound awareness of the company's internal business structure and utilizes it to best effect.'

Comment: You need an appropriate level of business awareness, especially if you are involved in project-based decision-making and are required to see the bigger picture. You also need to understand how tasks are subdivided into separate jobs, who reports to whom and who has authority to make decisions.

- **Commercial acumen**: 'The manager demonstrates broad knowledge and comprehension of the macro business environment, constantly looking for opportunities to maximize profitability.'

Comment: This competency tends to be more relevant in middle and senior management positions. However, a fair understanding of your company's products, services, strengths, weaknesses, marketplace, competitors, customers and so on is necessary. Equally, your awareness of costs and effective cash management can often make the difference between profit and loss on any given project. A reasonable feel for 'money management' is usually essential.

- **Customer focus**: 'The manager anticipates the needs of both internal and external customers, providing a superior quality service and constantly delighting them by exceeding their expectations.'

Comment: I don't disagree that this competency is crucial to competitive advantage. However, whether you need to constantly delight customers and exceed their expectations is debatable. Perhaps meeting expectations is more appropriate given the need to maximize profit. What do you think?

- **Decision-making**: 'The manager makes clear decisions based upon judgement of the best solution to a problem or situation.'

Comment: You often don't know the best solution until after the decision. Consequently, this is a competency that is only evaluated in retrospect – especially for managers in more senior positions. Naturally, good judgement is related to good solutions – you can't have one without the other.

- **Forward planning and organizing**: 'The manager thinks ahead in order to effectively organize workload. Prioritises activities, efficiently establishes appropriate courses of action and monitors progress, accomplishing goals on time.'

Comment: This cluster of 'bedrock' management abilities is critical to enable efficient management of resources. How far you need to plan ahead will depend on your managerial level, your agreed responsibilities, authority and accountability. Monitoring progress is clearly related to the need to apply performance management and work towards continuous improvement. See more about this subject in Chapter 4.

- **Initiative and innovation**: 'The manager actively influences events rather than passively accepting [sic]. Sees opportunities and acts on them, without being asked, in pursuit of the organization's goals.'

Comment: Like most competencies this one can have negative effects if poorly managed or implemented. For instance, consider the manager who often takes the wrong initiative or makes decisions without discussing them. Being able and willing to take the initiative is a valuable asset to your management and the company. Developing, and then using, your people's innovative ability often provides the difference between good and outstanding performance.

- **Interpersonal style**: 'The manager considers and responds appropriately to the needs, feelings and capabilities of different people in different situations.'

Comment: This competency is often underestimated or totally ignored. It is one that sits within the 'soft' area of management and has much to do with behaviour, feelings and the psychology of managing others. Chapter 2 provides additional comments and guidelines while Chapter 3 gives details of techniques that you can learn to use well.

- **Leadership**: 'The manager guides individuals or groups towards the accomplishment of tasks. Creates an environment where people are positively motivated.'

Comment: Clearly an important concept and one that combines the need to encourage and motivate your people to get things done. Leadership, why it is needed, and what you might expect from people if you give it, is discussed in detail in Chapter 2.

- **Persuasive negotiation**: 'The manager negotiates confidently, convincing others of a particular point of view. Influences the outcome of discussions.'

  Comment: Good management requires self-confidence and the ability to persuade others. However, its usefulness depends on the judgement of the persuader. You might have come across people who are very persuasive but are often wrong. You need to know who in your team normally provides sound judgement.

- **Problem analysis and solutions**: 'The manager diagnoses problems and thoroughly assimilates analyses and evaluates all available information. Develops effective solutions which are in the best interest of the organization. Owns problems until they are resolved.'

  Comment: Experience suggests that sufficient information is hardly ever available. Effective solutions can only be judged in retrospect. However, assessment and use of data, especially comparative data, is crucial to improving performance. The areas which you might wish to generate comparative and benchmarked data together with guidelines as to how you might use this information are given in Chapter 4.

- **Team working**: 'The manager willingly works with others and supports them in order to achieve the best results as a team, over and above individual success.'

  Comment: The age of managing by supporting your people rather than telling them what to do has arrived. Clearly, this description clarifies the main purpose of a team – to achieve a synergy, that is, the sum of the whole (the team) is greater than the sum of the individual parts (each member of staff/workforce).

- **Work standards**: 'The manager's actions are guided by a high need for integrity in all aspects of work and for reaching exceptional standards of performance.'

  Comment: Here, again, the need for quality, continuous improvement, performance measurement and management. As for integrity, you can probably recall situations when one or more of your people, or your immediate manager, seems to act/behave without integrity, perhaps leaving you feeling confused and annoyed. Integrity, by the way, simply means to act with honesty and consistency so that people (regardless of hierarchical level) can rely on you.

- **Written and oral communication**: 'The manager listens carefully to others and responds appropriately. He or she communicates clearly and effectively both orally and in writing, demonstrating the ability to communicate meaningfully in a variety of settings at all levels.'

Comment: Communication is often seen as the one competency in which managers and organizations continuously fail to achieve the desired performance. Ask any director – they will say the biggest problem in their company is one of poor communication. We all know how to communicate. However, ensuring the right communication is provided at the right time to the right people in the right way is a skill most of us can only seek to improve – but never master. This valuable managerial skill is discussed further in Chapter 3.

For convenience, why not use the table below to chart your self-assessment? Use a scale of 1 to 5, 1 being a competency that requires a lot of development and 5 being a competency that you feel you already have in abundance.

Rate yourself.

Self-assessment Chart: Competency Ratings

Competency	1	2	3	4	5
Adaptability					
Business awareness					
Commercial acumen					
Customer focus					
Decision-making					
Forward planning and organizing					
Initiative and innovation					
Interpersonal skills					
Leadership					
Persuasive negotiation					
Effective problem analysis and solutions					
Team working					
Work standards					
Written and oral communication					

''Tis a wise person who knows their limitations as well as their own abilities.' (Unknown philosopher)

Being a manager or reader who aspires to a managerial role, you probably could not resist self-assessing yourself against each of the above competencies – how did you do? Which of them do you need to improve? Have you any ideas as to how to improve them? Later chapters should help.

Many employees in the construction industry are self-employed and need only to ensure they possess the appropriate competencies to be personally effective. If you are in this position, you do not have to be concerned about ensuring and improving staff core competencies. However, if you are successful, it will not be long before you realize that taking on extra help is crucial to the firm's growth potential. Finding and employing appropriate qualities in the workforce is a hurdle too many embryonic businesses find difficult to handle and often stunts early company growth. How to recruit, select, develop and retain people will be dealt with in Chapter 3.

The knowledge economy

Managers in medium and large organizations often fail to capitalize and exploit to good advantage knowledge held within the organization.

The 'knowledge economy' is a term used to describe the importance of 'know-how' for future high-level performance and wealth creation. The idea suggests that companies will progressively rely on the existing knowledge and ability of employees to innovate, acquire and exploit new knowledge.

'Minds are like parachutes. They only function when they are open.' (Sir James Dewar)

As a resource to be exploited, a firm's intellectual/knowledge capital is not just about your employees' ability, but also a question of their enthusiasm and commitment. Your people and their intellectual capital is your organization's only appreciable asset. Consequently, organizations now recognize the need to work with 'creation – using the mind' as well as 'creation – using physical tools'.

Knowledge has always had value. In many ways, the idea of knowledge capital is not new. Exploiting knowledge has always been important to organizations, regardless of sector. You can develop your intellectual capital by developing your people and encouraging their commitment to the company. Unfortunately, vital knowledge often seems to 'walk out of the company door' as some employees (often the best people unfortunately for the manager) become disillusioned or decide to retire early. Of course, people do retire and must be able to do so. However, it is your job to ensure that your people do not retire their mind while they are still employed. Here are a few ways that can kill off people's enthusiasm, creativity and innovation:

How to kill off ideas.

1 Suggest that new ideas emanating from other people cannot be of any use. If they were useful, you would have thought of them in the first place.
2 Always challenge new ideas on the basis that they have not yet been tried out. Ask for several examples of them being successful while allowing competitors to use them first.
3 Always act as though you know more than your people – about everything. After all, you are the boss.
4 Criticize new ideas from others because supporting them might give them a career advantage. View all new offerings from people with suspicion.

5   If you pick up an idea from those around you, pretend it was yours in the first place. Never acknowledge your people's contribution.

6   If one of your ideas, or one that you have borrowed from someone else, turns out to be a problem, suggest that others are to blame.

7   Ensure that barriers to working relationships are formed and maintained between your people, your site, section, project or department and others.

8   Run hourly checks on the progress of everyone's work.

9   Ensure that highly qualified and creative individuals report their ideas in detail or, better still, ask them to provide a 50-page justification, give them more monotonous work, place absolute emphasis on the short term and call lots of meetings.

10 Subdue laughter and discourage social events.

Organizational success depends on many factors, some of which are beyond your control. Nevertheless, it has been too easy for managers to adopt the view that their staff have an obligation to do as they are told. Today, such an attitude is not useful. Some employees may never respond to good management, but they are in the minority. Working towards establishing a critical mass of enthusiastic employees will bear dividends.

Summary

This chapter has highlighted important forces driving today's construction industry. It has also offered some equally important ideas about how firms and you can adjust and respond effectively to external pressures. These areas are further developed in Chapters 2 through 5. As an incentive to read on, it is worth mentioning that the best construction organizations innovate, capture and exploit knowledge through the effective recruitment, selection, development and encouragement of people. They assist people development, ensure appropriate training, build teams (not just groups of people), implement processes that welcome communication across as well as up and down the company, ensure that managers support people and encourage new ideas and new ways of working, and make sure that ideas for improvements in performance are noted, communicated, recorded and discussed. Importantly, firms also need to apply a form of management that helps, or at least does not hinder, individuals and groups of individuals performing well. High performance outcomes require a better understanding of people. Chapter 2 will provide a few good and timeless guidelines.

Chapter 2

Improving People Performance: The Approach

Managers and leaders

Most practising managers suggest that management is concerned with bringing together resources, developing strategies, planning, organizing, coordinating and controlling activities in order to achieve agreed aims and objectives. In many respects, Chapters 3 and 4 adopt this view and concentrate on strategies and techniques to recruit and develop people, and to provide structures, policies and practice that help plan, coordinate and review people performance. Perhaps the difference between managers and leaders is that leaders do the right things and managers do things right. My own view is that managers should be interested in doing the right things as well as doing things right. What do you think?

Managers do the right things and do things right.

It might be a good idea at this stage if I provide a few generic descriptions of good managers and good leaders (see Tables 2.1 and 2.2). You are unlikely to wholeheartedly agree with any one description; however, as you read the descriptions in each column try to decide which one best describes the way you operate at work.

Manager characteristics	Leader characteristics
Administers	Innovates
A copy	An original
Maintains	Develops
Focuses on systems	Focuses on people
Relies on control	Inspires trust
Short-range view	Long-range perspective
Asks how and when	Asks what and why
Eye on the bottom line	Eye on the horizon
Imitates	Originates
Accepts the status quo	Challenges the status quo
Classic good soldier	Own person
Does things right	Does the right thing

Source: Based on Bennis (1990, p. 45).

Table 2.1 *Characteristics of managers and leaders according to Bennis*

Managers	Leaders
Plan and budget	Establish direction
Organize staff	Align people
Control and problem-solve	Motivate and inspire
Focus on order and predictability	Focus on change

Source: Kotter (1990a).

Table 2.2 *Activities of managers and leaders according to Kotter*

You will notice the subtle differences academics make between the two roles. Of course, what we are interested in is not academic debate. The crucial issue for any practising manager is how they should manage others in order for them to perform well. Do people in today's construction firms need good managers or good leaders?

Good managers might be described as fairly analytical, controlled, deliberate and orderly. They determine the scope of problems and consider business risk. They may seek markets, or at least be aware of them; they think about competition, follow visions and try to correct strategic weaknesses – mostly related to internal resources. Most managers use their authority, think logically, and administrate to seek uniformity and consistency; they desire stability and attempt to 'fasten things down'. They manage by setting goals and objectives, scrutinizing performance, concentrating on short-term results and reacting to variances in performance by reorganizing and refining work activity. Do you fit this description?

'If everything seems under control, you're not going fast enough.' (Mario Andretti)

Good leaders, on the other hand, are flexible, creative and innovative; they intuitively know the right things to do and they can spot windows of opportunity and pursue their vision. When problems arise they seek sufficient information and look for alternative solutions – they build on company strengths. They manage people by applying influence rather than force, they empower people and get results by enhancing employee competence, they inspire through personal communication and prefer informality and making good relationships with people inside and outside the firm. They develop people and set an example for others to follow. In general they are optimistic, they confront but do not create conflict, after explaining why improvements are necessary they demand improvement but ensure incentives and rewards. Their very presence has a positive effect on people.

Well, how did you get on? Which description best captures the way you see yourself at work? If your people answered for you, would they say that you have more leadership than management traits? Hopefully, they see your behaviour as their boss as in some way matching both descriptions.

'No person can be a great leader unless they take genuine joy in the successes of those under them.' (W.A. Nance)

Do firms operating in the construction industry, whether small or large, need managers or leaders? Well, by now you know what I think – they need both, and in many ways managers of departments, functions or project teams, regardless of size, can be leaders of their teams as well as managers. As indicated above, the best leaders use both management and leadership skills and abilities, depending on circumstances. So, are managers also leaders? Again you know my view – yes, they can be. Many people in their everyday working lives use both management and leadership skills in the correct mixture. Most importantly, very effective managers of people adopt leadership qualities. That is how they constantly motivate their people into high performance.

Of course, some of your people can be leaders without being operational managers. This fact is important to you, because you may rely on certain people within teams to take on the role of team leader. Equally, a person who is a manager may not be a leader. A person is a manager by virtue of holding a formal position that gives them positional power or authority. Consequently, if you are a manager and not a leader, your people will do as you say (most of the time) because you have authority. In constrast, a leader is determined by those who are led, not just by an official position.

Leadership in the workplace

In the workplace it is common to talk about managers and not leaders. Nevertheless, when I focus on excellence in people management, referring to leadership characteristics often proves useful in distinguishing between poor or average managers and best-case management. You may agree with me that the success or failure of a manager rests mainly on the shoulders of their staff. Generally speaking, unless you are a sole trader, if you try to succeed without the cooperation of your people, your efforts will most likely end in frustration, overwork, anxiety, stress and, usually, poor or, at best, average results. You get cooperation and superior work performance by applying leadership skills.

People can manage without leaders. Yet, whenever a group of people get together to perform a task, a leader normally emerges or is appointed. Ask most employees what they want of management, and they may respond that they want their managers to lead by example. However, ask people who their leader is and they will most probably be offended that you think 'they need to be led'. Let's be clear: leaders are not super all-knowing and special beings, and subordinates are not sheep waiting for the leader 'sheepdog' to give them some ideas as to what to do and where to go.

People refer to the process of leadership, what leaders say and do, and refer to typical leadership characteristics while assuming that we all share one common understanding. That is not true. Some descriptions from various publications and journals provide evidence of many differing views:

Leadership is the activity of influencing people to cooperate toward some goal which they come to find desirable.

The functions of leadership include: providing equipment, materials and supplies, development of personnel, planning work, directing activities, selecting methods, checking results.

Leadership is a system of organized methods of operation in controlling work performance.

Leaders in various ways guide, control, direct, counsel, advise, teach, influence, and help others in the conduct of their public and private lives.

Leadership on the job is summed up in the effect that everything a leader says and does has on the workforce ... Leadership involves securing [followers'] willing co-operation, their interest, and their desire to do the job the way [the leader] wants it done ... being ahead of the group, showing the way, finding the best path to [the leader's] objective.

Different definitions of leadership: Which one is most fitting?

Leadership is principally a task of planning, co-ordinating, motivating and controlling the efforts of others toward a specific objective.

Leadership is not an abstract essence. It is a function, an influence, and a relationship.

A leader is a person who is appointed, elected, or informally chosen to direct and co-ordinate the work of others in a group.

Well – there you have it! Is leadership more of a skill, or a task, or a series of functions, or a system of control, or more of a process, or perhaps to do with decisions, or an expression of personal qualities, or a service, or a relationship? Let me be clear; leadership is something that good managers will want to achieve. Put simply, to lead is to guide or show the way by going in front. A leader might therefore be defined as one who is followed by others. Perhaps far more importantly, leadership is the process of motivating as well as directing other people to act in particular ways to achieve specific goals. You will know when your leadership skills are working because your staff will have an extra enthusiasm to achieve the objectives you set. Moreover, others will see them as being highly productive – in comparison, that is, to the staff of other managers.

What makes a good leader?

It may be of interest that, in a classroom rather than building-site setting, it is common, when asking students about the characteristics of leaders, for prominent figures to be used to justify the importance of great vision and achievement. Historical biographies of great men and women such as Alexander the Great, Joan of Arc and Winston Churchill provide enticing support for the view that some people may be born with innate leadership characteristics. Supporters of this idea suggest that some people possess a natural ability to rise out of any situation and become great leaders. You might argue that leadership in the workplace is very different from leadership on the battlefield or when a country is in a state of war. Nevertheless, one thing is fairly certain, when managing people in a work setting, any simple connection between genes, biological influences and personal behaviour seems oversimplistic and tends to ignore the impact of experience, self-development, and context – including the building site.

If leadership ability is inherited, the selection and recruitment of managers as potential leaders would only focus on the candidate's parents and ancestors – evidence of work experience would not be valued. Moreover, if leaders are born and not developed, then high-performing people would always emerge regardless of the business context, their management ability or the company's willingness to recruit and select well, or coach, mentor, train, develop and appraise employees. Furthermore, attempts to improve performance would be a wasteful exercise. Such an idea should not be taken too seriously, so why, then, have I mentioned it? Simply because, in my experience, some managers manage their people based on this idea, and it prevents them from applying the person-management skills and techniques that lead to improved performance. I feel that it is far better to accept that the work environment, including management action, shapes people's behaviour and abilities and that every manager can improve the way they manage people regardless of innate characteristics.

Management and leadership style

Most managers support the idea that leadership or management style is fundamental to obtaining good performance from people. Style refers to how managers behave towards their staff. Some suggest that a supportive 'people' style leads to greater subordinate satisfaction, lower grievance rates and less conflict. A manager would be using a supportive style if they managed others on a day-to-day basis in a way that focused on ensuring that processes, information, communication and the like was supportive of the duties, responsibilities and motivations of their staff. Others suggest that adopting a participative management style strongly and positively enhances employee commitment. A manager using this style would make decisions based on a great deal of discussion with their staff and allow decisions to be changed or influenced as a result of that discussion. Perhaps a democratic leadership style can lead to higher levels of employee commitment. It may certainly be preferable to an authoritarian style where power is exercised solely by the manager.

They say that a picture is better than a thousand words. Have a look at Figure 2.1. Which illustration best describes the way your organization works and the way you manage? The one on the right depicts a conventional authority-based, top-down structure of operation. The one on the left suggests that managers should work to support the organization – and, of course, both support the customer.

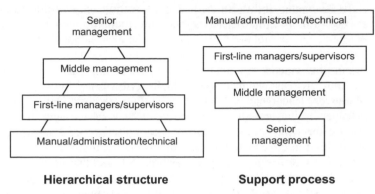

Hierarchical structure	**Support process**

Figure 2.1 *A different way of thinking?*

Given that your firm needs to develop a flexible, quick, responsive, opportunistic and supportive approach so that you can improve its competitive advantage, which structure would be the most effective?

What management style do you use most often?

How do you manage/lead your people? What style do you use? Try to choose from one of the following four styles and then read on to check whether further evidence supports your choice:

1 *Directive*: The leader gives specific directions and the subordinate does not participate.
2 *Supportive*: The leader is friendly and shows concern for subordinates.
3 *Participative*: The leader asks for suggestions but still makes decisions.
4 *Achievement-oriented*: The leader sets challenging goals and shows confidence in subordinate ability and willingness to perform well.

Managers who are able to use all four styles but use each at the right time, in the right way and in the right place tend to be more effective than a manager who adopts a rigid style. Of course, the trick is knowing when to use which style. The most effective style depends on the factors contained within specific circumstances and, consequently, the style used to manage employees may have to change – who said managing people was simple? As a general guideline, to improve performance and smooth the path towards achieving company goals, you should try to positively influence people by practising the different styles of leadership in different circumstances. Therefore, it is best to view leadership as a process that requires you to assess the specific situation and act accordingly – a continual dynamic process that your people generally see as balanced and *firm but fair*.

In addition to the need to use different leadership styles to suit the situation, I also keep in mind the need to use a generally balanced approach to work and people. For example, on an everyday basis, I try to give equal weight to my interest in getting the job done and encouraging people to do it well. You and your people have a clear job to fulfil to the best of your abilities, but, as their manager, you should not focus so heavily on performing well on the task at hand that you ignore people's concerns. There is a fair amount of evidence that adopting this balanced approach may bring the most success in maintaining high performance from people. Moreover, leadership is often described as the ability of a good manager to balance the extremes of a task-related and results orientation with a process-based concern for people. When you think about it, there is nothing new in this idea. It is simply common sense that the firm has a need to perform well and that people have individual and group-related needs that require attention in order for them to perform well. Your job is therefore to achieve a reasonable balance.

Managers do not exist in a vacuum; they are clearly affected by circumstances at work. For example, your chosen management style is probably affected by your organization's performance. Also, whether you realize it or not, the way you manage is influenced by what you think of your people. Most of us cannot do much about the economic conditions affecting our organization, but we can do something about what we think of our people. Having the right attitude towards people is important. Without it, we cannot manage people in a balanced way.

I frequently use a well-known idea to challenge manager perceptions. I am, of course, referring to McGregor's Theory X and Theory Y (1960) which suggests that the style managers adopt is caused by their attitudes to employees, and these attitudes are based on their view of human nature and behaviour. The two theories provide oversimplified, extreme but recognizable management views. As you work through the descriptions below, decide which theory most closely fits your view about people.

Theory X – a traditional 'carrot and stick' approach to management.

Theory X is offered as a traditional 'carrot and stick' approach to management. Its assumptions are as follows:

1 People are inherently lazy and dislike work.
2 People's natural goals run counter to those of the organization.
3 Because of their irrational feelings, people are incapable of self-discipline and self-control.
4 People can be divided into two groups. The first group fit the above assumptions, prefer to be directed, lack ambition but value security. The second group consist of those who are self-motivated, self-controlled and not dominated by their feelings. Therefore, they must assume management responsibility for the former.

According to Theory X, you are responsible for organizing the elements of production, money, materials, equipment and people in the interest of economic ends. Without the interventions of management, people would be passive or even resistant to organizational needs. The management of people must involve a process of directing, controlling and modifying employee behaviour. You must therefore persuade or coerce employees to conform.

You achieve this by means of reward (primarily financial) and punishment. If you adopt a Theory X view of your people, you are likely to use a directive authority style. Does this view match (or partially match) the way you manage your people? If not, do you know any people who seem to manage in the Theory X way?

Unfortunately, Theory X assumptions are not always useful for fulfilling the growing need for organizations to harness the creativity and goodwill of employees. I mentioned the need to develop and use people's knowledge and skills in Chapter 1. As a consequence, many jobs have become more complex, and organizations have come to expect, and even rely on, employee judgement, creative capacity, loyalty and increased commitment.

Theory Y – a more modern view of people and supportive management approach.

Of course, there will always be some employees who fit the Theory X notion very well. For those who do not, McGregor provides an alternative Theory Y approach to people management. Managers adopting a Theory Y approach believe the following:

1 People seek to be mature in their job.
2 People can learn to take responsibility, and are capable of self-direction, self-control and self-development.
3 People's motivations are normally at levels above security needs (more about this later).
4 Given the chance, employees will voluntarily integrate their own goals with those of the organization.

The management implications of adopting a Theory Y approach are substantial: your role and style changes to one of helping and supporting your employees to find meaning in their work and to make the most use of their abilities. Consequently, it may be more fruitful to imagine your people not as an unavoidable consequence of the process of the organization but, conversely, as the organization itself – as the source of high performance.

As you read the above, you probably decided which theory most closely fits you, your job and your firm. If you chose Theory X you are more likely to manage in a traditional way. Your relationship with employees is likely to reflect a traditional 'mutually dependent' exchange in which rewards are given for satisfactory completion of the work task. It involves you in exercising your legitimate authority in order to achieve organizational goals. This may all be very well, but the performance you are likely to get from your people will at best be average. In contrast, if you think Theory Y has something to offer, your next question might be 'How do I need to behave in order to transform average worker performance into high performance?'. Transformational leaders inspire and motivate their people through personal vision and energy, and share the following characteristics:

Transformational leaders: how they act.

1 *They identify themselves as change agents.*
2 *They are courageous.*
3 *They believe in people.*
4 *They are value-driven.*
5 *They are lifelong learners.*
6 *They have the ability to deal with complexity and uncertainty.*
7 *They are visionaries.*

(Tichy and Devanna, 1986, pp. 271–80)

The incentive to managers who aspire to be transformational leaders is that, in doing so, they can change the basic values, beliefs and attitudes of their people to a point at which their people are willing to perform beyond the minimum performance levels specified by the organization. This results in high-performing individuals and consequent high-performance company outcomes.

I make no apology for the above theoretical approach – after all, you may, like me, find that some well-chosen ideas encourage you to think about how you can improve. Nevertheless, what does all this mean to you and me in practical terms? In an attempt to single out what makes a good leader while avoiding references to any theoretical approaches, I conducted an inquiry among directors between 1993 and 2002. In this, I simply asked them to list the qualities of managers performing a leadership role that would most influence the performance of their company (see Table 2.3).

Qualities that influence company performance: how many do you recognize?

• Able to maintain integrity/honesty	• Interpersonal skills
• Good communicator	• Risk taker (measured)
• High stamina/energy	• Astute as to internal politics
• Visionary	• Charismatic
• High intellect	• Approachable
• Financial awareness	• Trustworthy
• Credible	• Friendly
• Quick learner	• Teambuilder
• Able to get the best out of people	• Motivated
• Enthusiastic	• Sense of humour
• Strategic thinker	• Good 'time manager'
• Challenging	• Able to delegate
• Maintains integrity	• Decisive

Table 2.3 *'Good' leadership characteristics: the directors' view*

The characteristics identified by directors confirm essential traits such as 'high intellect', 'quick learner' and 'motivated'. Their views suggest a leader should be, for example, approachable, friendly and able to maintain integrity – that 'integrity' word again! Moreover, the list confirms the importance of transformational characteristics such as 'challenging', 'visionary' and 'enthusiastic'. Experience suggests that managers wanting high performance should, on a day-to-day basis, develop and adopt the leadership behaviours and attitudes listed in Table 2.4.

• Nurture a positive yet flexible culture	• Be positive
• Serve and support people	• Search for cohesive solutions
• Behave as a partner, not a boss	• Elicit creativity
• Be inspirational	• Use emotional intelligence
• Develop people	• See simplicity
• Seek out potential in others	• Use empathy

Table 2.4 *Leadership behaviours and attitudes that encourage high performance from people*

The lists in Tables 2.3 and 2.4 are good general guidelines, but they are manager/leader views of leadership – what about other people's (potential followers') views? One important investigation (Taylor, 1962) simply asked people what they wanted from their manager/leader in order to work more effectively, and they came up with the following list:

1 *Thoughtfulness*: Treat people with courtesy.
2 *Impartiality*: Treat people with equal consideration and avoid favouritism.
3 *Honesty*: Behave with a sense of fair play and trustworthiness.
4 *Proficiency*: Illustrate and display technical and people-related skills.
5 *Person-knowledge*: Understand people's needs and behaviour.
6 *Control*: Accept the power that the leadership position offers.
7 *Courage*: Be positive and committed.
8 *Directness*: Provide feedback about people's performance – but always with tact.
9 *Decisiveness*: When the occasion fits, 'call the shots'.
10 *Dignity*: Do not oversocialize.
11 *People interest*: People need and expect to be 'put ahead' of the task.
12 *Helpfulness*: In the eyes of followers, the only real justification for a leader's existence is their ability and willingness to help followers attain goals and satisfy working needs.

Well, what do you think? Would your people come up with similar views? Would they say you currently manage like this? Would such a style be appropriate in your work setting? I leave you to answer these questions.

To briefly summarize, experience suggests that the idea that leadership ability has absolute links with ancestry and genealogy is a step too far. Nevertheless, while I was working as a personnel/human resource practitioner, so many employees commented that the 'style' of their manager affects their performance that, pragmatically, you should not ignore this idea. My personal preference is to balance styles rather than work to polarized extremes. The transformational leadership notion emphasizes the effect leaders can have on people. Its focus on the need to motivate people in order to improve performance has been well received in most companies.

I would suggest that organizational leadership is both a quality and a process; it involves managerial efficiency but concentrates on a leader effectiveness that results in willing followers highly committed to the goals and objectives provided by the leader. Today, it is commonly held that for companies to survive and prosper they are going to need a new generation of leaders – leaders not managers.

Leadership is a 'quality' of good managers and a 'process' by which to get the best from people.

A final, but important, aspect of good management is worth mentioning – that of establishing and developing trust. Your people are extremely unlikely to perform exceptionally if they do not trust you. Trust is something that cannot be requested, only given. Moreover, trust must be earned. You must earn the trust of your people by behaving with integrity and never forgetting their needs. How do you do this? Some answers are provided by considering two key, but related, management issues – worker commitment and work motivation – subjects discussed in the next section. Above all, try to remember that worker performance relies on the confidence your people have in you. This will be built up over a long time. Unfortunately, it can be quickly and easily destroyed – don't let that happen.

'The significant problems we face cannot be solved at the same level of thinking we were at when we created them.' (Albert Einstein)

Employee commitment: what does it look like?

As a manager you not only want your people to use their knowledge and skills, you also want them to be committed to what they do because that is how you get the best performance from them. But what does commitment look like? Would you recognize committed behaviour? This short section describes what commitment looks like.

Without employee commitment, outstanding work performance is impossible.

The key objective of all management is to develop and promote commitment. Commitment is important in gaining both quality and productivity improvements; it is the 'vital spark' demonstrated by some people and teams that makes them stand out as your best people.

Although you want your people to stay with the company and not take their strengths elsewhere – perhaps to competitors – a commitment to just stay with the company might not always be totally desirable. I imagine that you want more from your people than simple compliant behaviour that aids their continuous employment but may add little to the organization's performance. The commitment most valuable to you takes the form of your people wanting to remain in the organization because they have developed a positive attitude towards the organization and/or its leadership – you. This type of commitment is triggered when an employee can relate to, and agree with, the organization's objectives because they fit well with their own personal objectives and needs.

I asked several managers what they wanted from their people in terms of commitment, and they suggested the following:

It is not always advisable to retain all of the same employees.

It is extra effort that management require, not simply the continuance of what has been done before.

Compliance is only useful at certain times. When it becomes less useful is when we want employees to think for themselves or to benefit from creative ideas... creative ideas are becoming more important.

I hope you will agree that the kind of commitment you want to develop ends in your employees showing a willingness to put in a great deal of effort beyond that normally expected in their current job. You may also find that these people often say things suggesting that their job is important to them, that it makes good use of their abilities and that they get a great deal of satisfaction from it. They may even 'talk up' the organization and its managers as being good to work for and/or of being considerate to people.

Now that we have a fair understanding of the best form of commitment to look for, is it worth putting in management effort to encourage it? First, we consider the important link between commitment and job performance.

It is accepted that greater commitment leads to improved work and organizational performance. Most managers believe that real commitment from staff would dramatically improve the performance of their businesses. Interestingly, investigation has found a positive relationship between organizational commitment and output measures of performance, such as a change in operating profit and sales targets. Of course, people's commitment is influenced by management actions and behaviour. Moreover, employee satisfaction and commitment to the organization is linked, and employee satisfaction leads to improved organizational performance. So there you have it – the challenge and the promise of improved management and leadership leads to an improvement in work satisfaction, greater commitment to the job and improved company performance.

Various methods have been used by managers to improve their people's commitment to their job and to the firm. These include briefing groups and team briefings, acting as change champions or as role models, acting as change agents, using quality circles or holding quality improvement meetings, using and/or taking part in training and development and making better use of appraisal/

'Never mistake motion for action.'
(Ernest Hemingway)

Effort that boldly goes where you hope all your people will go.

performance reviews, improving the way teams work, building teams and so on. All rely on appropriate management action and behaviour. There is more about how you can use these techniques and ideas to your advantage in Chapters 3 and 4.

Do you like to be told what to do or do you prefer to be asked your opinion and be involved in decisions? Observation suggests that employees actively engaged in decision-making throughout the company have higher job satisfaction. Generally speaking, people are rarely motivated by being told what to do – people like you and me want to be involved.

No one wants to be told what to do!

You can involve your people by giving them appropriate information and asking them for their opinion – during team briefings, for example. You can also increase opportunities for employee involvement by allowing employees to offer information – for example, through suggestion schemes and quality improvement meetings – or by changing the relationship between you and your people through more participative leadership and perhaps greater informality.

Some investigations indicate that when techniques such as job enhancement, enrichment and employee involvement are used, an increase in job satisfaction occurs (see the discussion later in this chapter). In addition, organizations show an increase in profitability a short while after introducing such techniques.

'The difference between "involvement" and "commitment" is like an egg-and-ham breakfast: the chicken was "involved" – the pig was "committed".' (Unknown author).

People's attitudes towards employee involvement initiatives depend on, among other things, experiences they have had of employee involvement and work in general, management's approach to employee relations, and the recent and projected corporate performance of the organization. Involvement schemes are therefore as much affected by the prevailing work culture (the working environment – what it feels like to work in your firm) as they are sources of cultural change. Some company-wide strategies to implement new ideas such as empowerment and involvement schemes have been known to fail. Reasons for this include:

- Employees lack choice about participating in such initiatives.
- Employees lack trust in management.
- There is unequal status and unequal outcomes among employees.

There is far less doubt about the fact that good managers appear to be able to bring out additional energy from people – that 'vital spark' I talked about earlier. They do so by understanding and engaging with the motivational needs of their staff.

Motivation

Motivation is the process that directs your people's work energy. It is the drive behind your own and your people's wish to satisfy 'workplace' wants and needs. This drive causes people to behave in a specific manner aimed at satisfying certain goals. Your job is to make sure your people's motivation is directed at satisfying the goals and/or objectives of the organization. But, in order to be effective, your people's motivations must also be satisfied. Put simply, to get the type of commitment mentioned earlier, both individual and company needs must be satisfied at the same time – a neat trick, but not impossible.

Well-motivated employees are central to high organizational performance. This is especially so for firms that operate in rapidly changing market environments where competition and the need for constant innovation and continuous improvement are intense. Hence, it is a crucial issue for organizations operating in the construction and/or property management industry. Of all the functions a manager and potential leader performs, motivating potential followers is arguably the most difficult. Therefore, consideration of work motivation and management action that helps develop and sustain employee commitment is essential.

The term 'motivation' comes from the Latin word *movere*, which simply means 'to move'. However, willing behaviour towards the satisfaction of particular goals suggests more than movement. It is worth mentioning that we cannot see a motive because it involves feelings. However, we can infer what motivation another person requires satisfaction from or what motivation they are currently gaining satisfaction from. To assist our understanding of the reasons for others' behaviour we are likely to use our own experiences, perceptions and judgement.

It is possible an individual may have more than one motive in operation at any one time. Moreover, motivations may change. For example, as an employee's income increases, money may become less of a motivational factor. Moreover, as an employee gets older, interesting work might become more of a motivator. However, although people may differ as to the type or intensity of their motivation, groups of individuals share similar motivations. This is good news for managers. It means that all we need to do is provide the right work environment so that shared motivations can be satisfied. If we manage to do this, then we can expect better work performance. What we need to know is: what are the likely shared motivations and what can we do to make sure they are satisfied? This section of the book intends to answer these two questions.

Let me explain what I think motivation in the workplace is all about. Motivation is an internal and individual process that guides, directs and/or drives behaviour towards the satisfaction of valued, and perhaps prioritized, needs or wants that can be enhanced or subdued by the work environment. Such a view recognizes that motivation is under the control of the individual person but that their personal work experience will affect, or even govern, their behaviour. When we say that a person is not motivated, what we are really stating is that a person is not motivated to do what we want them to do. They are motivated, but their motivation is directed at other things – for example, to save their energy for different pastimes and (unfortunately for their manager) do as little work as possible. You must therefore find ways, activities, work practices, a suitable management style or work interventions that assist in motivating employees.

Motivational theory for the practising pragmatic manager

In this book I am only interested in theory if it can assist company performance. Fortunately, carefully selected concepts can aid understanding and provide support for certain management approaches and action that help improve employee performance.

Managers usually want a certain level of job performance from an individual, and motivation is seen as one stage in a sequence of stages leading to that level of performance (see Figure 2.2).

A bit of theory coming up – but only to help your understanding.

MOTIVATION ➡ BEHAVIOURAL CHOICE ➡ LEVEL OF PERFORMANCE

Figure 2.2 *From motivation to level of job performance*

Many attempts have been made to gain a greater understanding as to why people decide to do 'the things they do' and 'adopt attitudes they adopt'. The former is often categorized as 'content' theories and the latter as 'process' theories. These theories have been subsequently used as a basis for managing. I and many of my colleagues bear these theories in mind on a day-to-day basis because they provide some welcome structure or 'scaffolding' to help us manage our people. The theories that follow have been chosen on the basis that they have affected the theory or practice of managing in organizations. They are also important to understanding the source of your employee's work energy and, when used correctly, as a means to improving employee commitment and work performance.

Need (content) theories

The idea of need is basic to explanations of employee behaviour. Need theory is based on the premise that individuals will try to behave in a way that satisfies an activated need. Table 2.5 gives a list of needs.

Need	Description
Achievement	The need to attain perceived difficult goals
Affiliation	The need to associate with others
Acquisition	The need to gather belongings
Aggression	The need to deride and blame others
Autonomy	The need to be independent
Blame-avoidance	The need to behave in a conventional manner
Deference	The need to admire a person in authority
Dominance	The need to control
Exhibition	The need to draw attention to oneself
Nurturance	The need to help others
Order	The need to organize and arrange things
Recognition	The need to receive credit for one's actions

Source: Murray (1938, p. 73).

Table 2.5 *People's needs*

What makes you work harder at work – is it any of these needs?

Have a look through the list of needs in the table. Which ones do you need to satisfy in your work? Some needs are clearly important to most people – the need for 'recognition' for instance. This is so important that I have dedicated a separate section to it later in this chapter. Other needs may be more specific to certain individuals – for example, the need for 'exhibition', to draw attention to oneself. This need is most likely to be more important to extraverts – perhaps some salespeople, architects or trainers. Certain inborn needs, such as needs for 'achievement' and 'autonomy', can be used by managers to set realistic but stretching goals and targets and to 'allow' or 'delegate' additional responsibility. Clearly, you have a responsibility to try to guess what drives each of your people.

Make a list of people around you in your team, or on your building site. Using the above list and from experience of their behaviour, write down, for each person, what you think are their primary or most likely motivations.

An old idea about motivation that has stood the test of time.

On the same theme, Maslow's (1943) 'hierarchy of needs' illustrates an order of priority needs. This is a useful listing because there are several needs clustered around just five headings, so I can usually remember them without looking in books.

Level 1 – Biological/physiological/basic needs: Air, thirst, hunger, sleep, warmth, sex.

Level 2 – Safety needs: Protection, freedom from pain, security, order, law, stability.

Level 3 – Belongingness/social needs: Love, friendships, work groups, family, affection.

Level 4 – Esteem/ego needs: Self-respect; confidence, independence, achievement, respect from others, reputation, status, recognition, attention, importance, appreciation.

Level 5 – Self-actualization needs: To fulfil one's potential.

Maslow suggests that a need would only become a motivator if it were not satisfied. Furthermore, attention would focus on the most basic need that is unsatisfied. This interpretation suggests that an employee would not pursue the next higher-order need in the hierarchy until a current, lower need was satisfied. Clearly, if you are starving the need for esteem is far less relevant. Similarly, it is difficult (if not impossible) to expect anyone to be motivated to achieve extensive performance targets if they are having problems in their marriage or if their house has just been repossessed.

In many organizations today, at least in the Western world, basic and safety needs are normally satisfied as part of the work environment. This means that you, as manager, should really be able to concentrate on levels 3 to 5. Level 3 suggests that you should think about forming appropriate work groups and teams. Working with others can be motivational especially if the team is well formed and you, as manager, build your team. Of course, you need to know how to build teams, and I will cover this important subject in Chapter 3.

In my opinion, level 4 needs are the most important for getting commitment and improving performance. Esteem needs are based on a person's need to value themselves, to have self-respect or self-esteem and, importantly, to receive respect from others, especially influential others – that is, you, as their manager. Although we talk about the need for people to reach level 5 and satisfy their potential, I don't know anyone who would say that they have accomplished it. I suppose if you are achievement-oriented, you never quite get there. Most of us would be very content remaining at high level 4 status.

Employee satisfaction

In 1966 a leading academic and adviser to management across the world produced factors that he stated were causes of satisfaction and dissatisfaction at work. This theory is probably the best and most useful for managers wanting to improve the performance of their people. The categories are constantly used by trainers/tutors and lecturers in attempts to explain aspects of work motivation. It is an attractive theory for management and students because it is easy to understand, provides a common-sense guide to possible practical interventions and is easy to remember. I have challenged different groups of managers to criticize or add to the categories, but all agree that, as a guideline to what motivates employees, the Herzberg categories offer managers specific recommendations about how to improve employee motivation and commitment (see Figure 2.3).

Satisfied employees are normally highly effective workers.

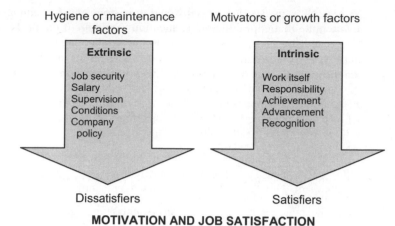

Source: Drawn after Herzberg (1966).

Figure 2.3 *Herzberg's motivators and hygiene factors*

Similar to Maslow's lower-level needs, 'hygiene or maintenance factors' include working conditions, salary and relationships with other workers. The other group, 'motivators or growth factors', is associated with satisfaction. The motivation factors complement Maslow's esteem and self-actualizing higher-order needs.

From a practical standpoint, the factors mentioned in this model are those over which you, as a manager, have at least some control. Managers wishing for well-motivated and committed people must first make sure that 'hygiene factors' do not distract their people from experiencing motivational satisfiers. For instance, it is clear that if you and the firm cannot provide some job security, a fair salary and good person management and supervision, getting well-motivated and committed people will be a problem.

The need to consider health and safety was outlined in Chapter 1. For example, you should ensure that:

- safety is designed into systems of work
- general rules are available on safe working habits
- special rules exist for people working at a height, in confined spaces, on electrical equipment and so on
- safety audits and inspections take place
- protective equipment is provided
- occupational health and safety arrangements are comm-unicated and appropriate training and education are provided
- an effective system is in place for reporting all accidents causing damage or injury
- appropriate records and statistics are kept and you analyse health and safety performance.

Your role is to develop or assist the development of health and safety policies and procedures, perhaps with the help of medical and safety advisers. At a supervisory/first-line management level, you must keep a constant watch for unsafe conditions and/or work practices. Look out for poor or defective working conditions such as:

- unguarded or inadequately guarded machinery
- defective plant and materials
- poor lighting or glare
- congested layouts
- unsafely designed premises, machinery, plans or processes
- overloading of machines
- inadequate ventilation or means of extracting fumes in a toxic environment.

When hygiene factors are satisfied to the point that they are no longer a cause of dissatisfaction, then you must work to improve motivators such as making sure that jobs can be satisfying – providing tasks within jobs that allow for a sense of achievement. What might this entail? First, each job must be designed so that it satisfies the organizational requirement for productivity, operational efficiency and quality of product or service. Second, it must satisfy the needs of the individual in terms of interest, challenge and a sense of achievement. You might wish to 'check out' your people's jobs against a variety of measures:

Assess your own and your people's jobs against this simple criteria.

1 Does each job provide a variety of tasks?
2 Does each job provide a degree of autonomy? Do job-holders have some control over the setting of their own goals?
3 Does each job provide an opportunity for the job-holder to use his or her abilities?
4 Does the job-holder receive feedback about their job and their performance in the job?
5 Does the job-holder think their task is important?

One sure way of stopping your people from being motivated and committed to you, the company and their team is to allow them to perceive their jobs as boring and/or not essential. Notice that I use the word 'perceived'. It is important for you, as manager, to realize that a job that provides satisfaction at one time for an individual may be seen as boring and not essential at another time. The job may have remained the same, but the individual may have outgrown the job or may have simply become so attuned to its requirements that it no longer serves any motivational interest – the job has lost value for the individual over time. To illustrate, let me tell you about my bathroom tiling project. I decided to do the tiling myself because my tiler continually let me down. You know the situation, 'I'll be there next week' – he never came. After six weeks of excuses ranging from, 'My last job has gone very wrong', 'My wife is complaining she never sees me', 'I need a holiday' (and he took two weeks to have one), 'It's such a big job I need to find two weeks when I haven't got any other work' to 'I've hurt my back', I decided to do the tiling myself. For the first three days, I enjoyed it – two walls completed and it didn't look too bad. I stood back with pride to survey my own work while my wife looked on admiringly and a neighbour asked for a quote – was I in the wrong job? Then it got complicated, working around waste-pipes, changing the radiator, and knowing that it would take another two weeks to complete the job. My enthusiasm slowly died. By the tenth day I did not want to see another white tile, cutting had become more than a chore, I had started dreaming about tiles (or were they nightmares?) and, just think, I still had to do the grouting. I won't go on, but will simply say that if my job was tiling, I would have lost interest.

Let me say that I know very few people who would say their job is always interesting. However, jobs should hold the promise of being intrinsically motivational. In other words, people should be motivated by the intrinsic content of the job; the job itself should provide the means by which your people receive satisfaction. This is important because it helps them meet their goals and work needs. If you have the opportunity to design or redesign jobs, you might first think about how you make sure each job fully uses the abilities of the job-holder. Second, you might design jobs so that the job-holder has a degree of autonomy – is able to use their discretion or at least have some self-control and responsibility. Third, you can, and should, design jobs so that they provide an opportunity for your people to do several tasks – give people a little variety to offset possible boredom. Finally, to reassure the job-holder, make a point of giving some positive feedback, allow them to go on a training programme to see how their job fits into the total project, or indeed into the company, and why it is important. There is more about the importance of training in Chapter 4.

Can you improve job satisfaction by trying out a few of these techniques?

Some ideas on aiding job variety have been well received. They are:

- *Job rotation*: This idea is fairly obvious – but not always so when you are in the thick of everyday problems. Just like asking the CEO to empty the rubbish, getting people to experience other people's jobs can have demonstrably positive outcomes and assist personal development. It can also reduce monotony, increase variety and remove some of the 'grass is always greener on the other side' view that most of us feel from time to time. Of course, you may decide that continuous job rotation is a good idea to prevent monotony, in which case you may want to organize a job rota system, although this is more difficult if the jobs themselves require specific expertise and/or qualifications.
- *Working in teams*: The importance and characteristics of teams will be described in Chapter 3. For now, think about how your people might work together in autonomous work groups or self-managed teams. Are they able to complete jobs without

too much management/supervision? Would their work effort and overall performance improve if they worked in a team environment and team culture?

- *Empowerment*: This idea is usually linked to the self-managed team approach and is now seen as crucial if the firm is to be flexible and responsive to market/customer needs. The term 'empowerment' is used to describe the process of devolving responsibility to its lowest possible level within the organization. Empowerment programmes can lead to major reductions in cost. The approach is also seen as motivational in the sense that empowered people are inherently satisfying their need for self-esteem – one of the important motivators mentioned above. However, in my experience, you need to be careful when empowering your people to work without supervision. They need to have the combined skills and appropriate knowledge to complete the team task without supervision, and you must be content to delegate responsibility and authority to them. Remember, empowerment does not work well if people are given extra work to do and the responsibility to achieve good results, but are given little authority and receive very little support from you when or if things go wrong.
- *Job enlargement*: There may be times when your people would respond favourably to doing some extra tasks – although I don't know of many who openly admit to being underworked! Nevertheless, if your people are bored doing the same old job, can you inject a little more challenge into the job content? Job enlargement might be a possibility if your people are involved in jobs that seem a little disjointed – they are not complete jobs. You may be able to put tasks together in such a way that what were fragmented tasks are now complete jobs.
- *Job enrichment*: You might be able to enrich certain jobs not by adding more tasks but by replacing more mundane tasks with others that carry more interest and/or responsibility. You may also be able to use 'current' tasks but add more responsibility and/or interest – for example, by giving greater control and responsibility for monitoring variances in costs. Of course, if appropriate and available, you may offer some people the chance of doing more interesting jobs that require greater use of their skills and knowledge. The new job may involve more pay, but not necessarily so. It may simply be the next step in personal and/or professional development.

Using a mixture of the above ideas helps maintain your people's interest in their own and other people's jobs and, consequently, I would advise you to think about how you might use them. Of course, you do not have to think big. Some of the best management ideas only involve a few small, but appropriate, job changes. Also, don't forget that many, if not most, individuals want to advance in their careers. Whilst everyone cannot become the managing director, there are things you can do, as a manager, that people will see as being supportive of career advancement. Examples might be developing your employees' competence or competencies (mentioned in the previous chapter), listening to their ideas and making sure they get recognition for new and useful ways of working, encouraging personal development and training, taking the role of a mentor to new employees, and conducting career counselling sessions as part of the performance management process. The manager as trainer, mentor and coach is discussed in Chapter 3.

Would any of the above have helped me do my tiling job? Well, yes and no. If I was trained to do some of the rewiring (under supervision), it would have made the job more satisfying. I can definitely say that I did not want the job to be enlarged, especially if it meant putting up more tiles. However, it would have been far less boring if I could have worked with someone rather than on my own. In the end, I have to admit that if my job was tiling, I would be in the wrong job, which says a lot about making sure you recruit the right person for the job in the first place. Furthermore, now that my wife has had a chance to really look at my less than perfect workmanship, she would agree.

All of the person- and/or job-related ideas mentioned can satisfy common job-related work motivations. For example, working in teams provides additional social contact – a natural human need. Equally, job enrichment, job enlargement and empowerment offer the opportunity for greater responsibility, achievement and improved self-esteem.

Most people agree that the Herzberg categories exist in most organizations. Generally, the two-factor model identifies important drives for people working within organizations. A common misinterpretation of Herzberg's theory is that pay is unimportant because it is not categorized as a motivation factor. But pay and salary is clearly important. Herzberg does argue the importance of pay, but as a hygiene rather than as a motivation factor – it is something that needs to be seen as fair. Hence the general use of market-based pay scales. I currently help manage a budget of £30 000 000, and over 70 per cent of this goes towards employee pay. However, I have very little opportunity to alter or adjust payments even though I have introduced a rewards and incentives policy – a form of performance-related pay. This means that I cannot rely on pay to enable high performance. You may be in a similar position. Nevertheless, if you, as a manager, are seen to provide more benefits than burdens for your employees, they are more likely to perform well. Benefits, that is, that are not directly pay-related. Experience shows that a clear difference between managers and leaders is that leaders understand which incentives are most valued and act accordingly.

Rewards and incentives

There is fair evidence that employee commitment is affected by rewards – I'm sure you would acknowledge this. However, whilst I accept that money is an incentive to all who have to work for a living, relying on money alone to motivate and get commitment to improved performance is very unlikely to succeed. Nonetheless, I need to mention performance-related pay (PRP) and how it can fit within a performance management system.

Your view and your people's view of what motivates them may be different – not a good starting point for performance improvements.

The whole point of providing pay for performance is that additional financial rewards can be given to people who perform well; it therefore acts as an incentive. Payment is based on an agreed rating system that you use to give some people extra payments. Although the operation of performance-related pay may vary, a typical element of a PRP scheme is that part of the pay structure is designed to be flexible. It is this part that you can use at your discretion. For example, you might rate each of your people on a scale ranging from exceptional performance to being ineligible for performance-rated pay. High-performing people will receive a greater percentage of the budget allocated for distribution via the PRP scheme. Before giving my opinion about PRP, I offer a few obvious advantages and disadvantages of such schemes.

Arguments for PRP:

- It seems fair to reward people according to their contribution to the company.
- It is a means of ensuring everyone understands the performance imperatives of the firm.
- It works as an incentive because money is perceived by many as still the best motivator of people and therefore performance.
- Ratings used to assess performance can help people know where they stand.
- Ratings also provide a convenient means of summing up judgements so that high and low performance can be easily justified.

Arguments against PRP:

- It is questionable whether pay is a motivator.
- It can be difficult to measure individual performance objectively, especially in company settings that rely on teamwork and cooperation and where the performance of any one individual or team relies heavily on others outside the immediate working environment – typical in the construction industry.
- Because ratings tend to be both subjective and inconsistent, unfair assessments of each individual, or even each team, may be made.

- It can make individuals and teams focus narrowly on the task identified by their manager as that which will give them most rewards. This might be fine where a task is well defined and a clear well-bounded performance measure has been agreed and applied (see a further discussion about performance measures in Chapter 4). It does not work as well when achieving the task requires a degree of flexibility – perhaps in relation to client wishes.
- Undue emphasis on individual performance might affect teamwork, and undue emphasis on team performance rather than on the need for teams to interact, cooperate and communicate can result in poor performance.
- Ratings used to assess performance can be a gross oversimplification.
- Ratings are often based on subjective judgements so consistency between two or more ratings is often problematic. Just think of two or three peer group managers – do they all see performance the way you do? Try a simple ratings exercise with your peers and check whether you agree. Unless you are rating something highly quantifiable – say, aspects of quality – disagreements can occur.

The one strong advantage is that it seems intuitively, morally and operationally right to reward people for the effort they put into their job and the contribution they make towards overall performance. By operating a PRP scheme, all workers are left in no doubt that good or high performance matters to the company and that the company thinks good performance should matter to each individual employee.

You may have experience of managing in a company that operates a PRP scheme and perhaps be aware of some of its drawbacks. You may also agree that pay is not a motivator; it is only something that, if not appropriate or acceptable, can be a cause of dissatisfaction. There is little evidence that people are motivated by their expectations about the rewards they will get from PRP schemes. Of course, there may be other reasons for this other than simply being unmotivated by financial rewards. For example, pay from a PRP scheme may be too insubstantial to motivate people.

More important than the debate as to whether pay is a crucial motivator is the fact that there are inherent difficulties in measuring performance in a suitable and agreeably objective way. This is especially so in jobs where the performance of the job-holder is strongly influenced by things that are either beyond their control (for example, economics or market trends) or are subject to the effort or influence of other people. Many believe that most jobs today cannot be singled out in any objective way from the effect of other people's performance – teamworking is an obvious example.

There is also a great danger that people will only concentrate on the measures used to assess performance. Of course, if the measures are absolute and all-encompassing (that is, they cover every aspect, activity, target area, behaviour and applied competency involved in the make-up of the job) there is less of a problem but, as you can imagine, that's not always a simple or cheap process. The administration and manager's time required to enable clear measures and targets carries a cost. Moreover, targets can change frequently, especially if your business has to operate in a very dynamic marketplace where new products and service solutions emerge on a regular basis. All this is not to say that performance targets have little purpose; as will be argued in Chapter 4, they are crucial to enabling improved performance. However, it is doubtful whether, when trying to apply measures to pay – it being a very emotive subject – the clarity required so that both manager and employee can feel comfortable and confident with them may not always be possible or cost-effective.

PRP can lay too much emphasis on individual performance. You may say, quite rightly, that that is what the scheme is supposed to do. Unfortunately, most people work as part of one or more teams, and PRP can reduce teamwork, innovation, sharing of knowledge and so on. In many ways it urges individuals to act competitively with other people – not a good idea if you are relying on the extra something that results in unexpectedly high performance that teams (rather than individuals or groups of individuals) can provide. More about the value of teamwork can be found in Chapter 3.

My opinion about PRP is based on my own experience of schemes that were introduced too quickly and without enough thought. Your experience may be very different. Of course, where the job is well designed, well defined and results simple to monitor and calculate, when schemes can measure performance accurately, when people view them as being fair, and when there is trust between employers and managers, then PRP can work successfully. In reality, this is often a tall order and I am concerned that introducing schemes on a broad scale makes it more difficult to gain collective commitment from people – many jobs today rely on teamwork and many jobs are simply not simple enough.

Some manual and/or shop-floor jobs where pay or part of an individual's or team's pay is related to the number of items they produce or process or the time they take to do a defined task – for example, laying a brick, fitting a window or plumbing in a sink – can benefit from incentive or payment-by-results schemes. When the scheme is based on the number of items or units of production, it is often referred to as piecework. When the measurement is time, payments usually follow a work measurement process. Payment is made depending on the 'actual time' taken with the 'standard work measured time' allowed to complete the task. As mentioned earlier, payment to individuals might not be helpful when teamwork is required or when you need your people to think for themselves and be innovative. However, incentive or payment-by-results schemes for teams whose task is measurable can encourage motivation, and peer group pressure from within the team can urge less efficient workers to improve their performance.

One final method of payment worthy of mentioning is measured daywork whereby pay is fixed on the agreement that people will maintain a given level of performance over a period of time, thereby reducing the effect of short-term fluctuations on the outcome. Incentive payments are normally agreed in advance of work being carried out. The advantage of this kind of arrangement is that you are able to directly link incentives with a required level of performance from your people. The disadvantages are that the agreement may take a lot of negotiation with employees and trade unions and it requires careful planning involving effective job evaluation and work measurement, efficient production/project planning and control and efficient inventory (stock) control systems. These requirements have led to firms turning to more simple systems that have the benefit of being flexible, such as an agreed day rate topped up with team bonuses. More common payments/ financial allowances would include payment for shiftwork, stand-by and call-out allowances and, of course, overtime payments.

It is likely that your organization pays different wages/salaries for certain individual skills. National Vocational Qualifications (NVQs – mentioned in Chapter 1) are a means of defining and assessing skill competence levels. Clearly, pay linked to skills is a useful incentive to people to increase their skill level. Of course, you as a manager also hold a great deal of responsibility for ensuring that your people use their skills to improve performance. Skill-based pay can be linked to NVQ competence levels and modules. For example, your company can choose certain skill-based modules or clusters (or sets) of modules that they see as crucial and that they are willing to reward with extra payments. The training can be accredited under the NVQ scheme or, alternatively, it can be certified by the company or a further or higher education institution. Your company may also be willing to extend this idea if the individual wishes to improve their knowledge of, for example, business skills, money management, marketing and so on. Chapter 4 gives more detail on training and development.

Other forms of pay-related incentives and rewards include team pay schemes, profit-sharing, profit-related pay (where part of pay is directly related to profits) or share option schemes (if your firm is quoted on a stock market) whereby you and your people might receive shares. Of course, should the company perform well, you can receive share dividends (less tax) and/or benefit from a potential increase in the market price of the share.

Moving on from pay, non-financial rewards or simply benefits from being employed might include security, appropriate and acceptable conditions of service, the employment contract and working conditions and company pension schemes.

Arguably, pension schemes are the most important employee benefit; they certainly grow in importance – especially when you get to my age. There is little doubt that occupational pension schemes attract and help retain high-quality people. When first introduced, the few participating companies were looked on as special organizations that showed great concern for the long-term needs of their employees. Today, these schemes are, thankfully, more commonplace. Any scheme – but especially a good scheme – will help retain your best people. There is more information about how to retain your best people in Chapter 4.

Other important allowances that might attract good people include a relocation allowance to enable people who currently live outside a reasonable commutable distance to join your company. Subsistence allowances that allow payments for accommodation, meal costs, training and course fees also help sustain satisfaction with the company.

One reason why common intrinsic motivation factors might have been overlooked is that some managers hold a different view as to what might motivate workers – different, that is, to what your people think. For convenience, Table 2.6 shows the lists I use with senior managers attending the Diploma in Directorship at the University of Salford to illustrate different worker and manager perspectives.

	Workers' view of workers' motivation		Managers' view of workers' motivation
1	Interesting work	1	Good salary
2	Recognition	2	Security
3	In the know	3	Personal development
4	Security	4	Working conditions
5	Good salary	5	Interesting work
6	Personal development	6	Empowerment (discretion)
7	Working conditions	7	Loyalty
8	Loyalty	8	Recognition
9	Social support	9	Social support
10	Empowerment (discretion)	10	In the know

Source: Based on Couger and Zawacki (1980).

Table 2.6 *Motivation: workers' and managers' perspectives (Couger and Zawacki)*

Couger and Zawacki's study suggests that managers consider safety and instrumental security needs as key to worker motivation. Workers, however, appear to favour needs more commonly associated with a combination of security, emotional, social and esteem needs. In particular, the motivational factor 'recognition' is conspicuously weighted differently. Another investigation by Kovach (1987) reveals a similar finding (Table 2.7).

Workers' view of workers' motivation		Managers' view of workers' motivation	
Recognition	First priority	Good salary	First priority
Good salary	Sixth priority	Recognition	Eighth priority

Source: Based on Kovach (1987).

Table 2.7 *Motivation: workers' and managers' perspectives (Kovach)*

If there is anything a manager can do on a day-by-day basis to improve people performance beyond expected levels, it is the application of recognition.

If we accept that workers were telling the truth about the intensity of what motivates them, the difference lies with management interpretation of what motivates workers. Clearly, management views of what motivates workers, at least in the Western world, is probably built on industrial–employee relations whereby trade union–company disputes focused on, or were settled by, pay bargaining. Constant attention to pay issues might have become the norm. Consequently, managers may have overlooked the importance of motivational factors more closely related to social needs, such as recognition. Do you?

Figure 2.4 represents my view of various forms of recognition that you might successfully apply.

ADVANCED FORM	NATURAL ACKNOWLEDGEMENT
PERSONAL DEVELOPMENT	MORALE SUPPORT
CONSIDERATION IN PROCESS, DECISION AND POLICY	
ACTIVE LISTENING	PRAISE

COMMON FORM	AUTHORITY	EMPOWERMENT
EQUITABLE SYSTEMS	TASK DEVELOPMENT	
RESPONSIBILITY	INVOLVEMENT	

BASIC FORM	PAY AND REWARDS

Figure 2.4 *Forms of recognition*

In business, recognition takes place when employees perform well – at least, it makes sense that it should. Recognition in this sense is unlikely to be given to employees who do not perform well; it is also something that you can provide or withdraw at will.

Obviously, recognition is often seen as synonymous with pay. However, you might also include recognition in the form of:

- titles
- formal commendations and rewards
- favourable mention in company publications
- freedom concerning job duties
- private, informal recognition for a job well done
- challenging duties
- varied, interesting work
- important, meaningful duties and responsibilities
- having influence in setting goals and making decisions.

Some management roles would naturally attract, or make possible and achievable, many of the above items of recognition. Other employees, however, may not be so gratified. Reward and recognition by means of the 'job itself' is less likely to be attractive to employees who hold a job that does not involve important, challenging, meaningful duties.

Perhaps important for any manager to acknowledge is motivation related to the need for esteem (level 4 in the Maslow hierarchy) – for instance, rewards such as a feeling of being appreciated, receiving positive reinforcement and recognition, being treated in a considerate manner, and being given the chance to use and achieve using one's own abilities. Let me clarify.

Generally speaking, I think the essence and foundation of what it means to feel recognized within the firm is relatively untapped and often missed by managers. To explain: the act of recognition is more than a list that you can use as a reward for good performance. Although few would deny the importance of receiving money and benefits, recognition involves less tangible but nonetheless important elements. In principle, what I call the act of applying 'natural recognition' is simple and, in my experience, critical in obtaining high performance from people. It involves thinking and asking questions – questions that enquire about my employee's needs and values – and acting upon information in a supportive way. Perhaps you are a parent. If so, you will know that recognition by you, being an influential figure within your child's world, is both an essential developmental feature and a natural occurrence – above all, it can help motivate your child to try to do better. One way of killing a child's enthusiasm is always to criticize their work, their abilities on the football or hockey pitch, their dress sense and so on.

I realize that parenting is a long way from the work environment. Nevertheless, I have found the use of support, consideration, development and simple, but continuous, acknowledgement of people's existence works in the work setting and is definitely the way to apply 'natural recognition'. Such aspects might include, but go beyond, social rewards such as friendly greetings, 'one-off' compliments and formal acknowledgement of achievement. Importantly, natural recognition can occur before, during and after good performance. For those with an academic bent, I have provided a working definition. As you read through the description think about whether the application of natural recognition could improve your people's performance – although, of course, it needs to be applied in a natural and uncontrived way.

Recognition in the workplace involves the acquisition of financial and non-financial rewards but, in essence, feeling recognized relates to the value an individual places on the basic need to be acknowledged and considered by influential others within the organization.

Summary

To summarize this section on motivating your people, it seems clear that each motivational factor is in some way under your control – or at least there for you to influence. It is equally clear that leaders wishing to enthuse, and develop a high level of commitment from, their people should consider the use of motivational factors such as recognition, praise, self-esteem and so on. Significantly, the need for self-esteem is directly related to the motivational factor of recognition.

Some common-sense guidelines might include the following:

- People like to be noticed – so notice them.
- People want to be appreciated – so pay attention to them and say thanks.
- People want a safe place to work – so provide one.
- People want to know what is expected of them – so give them a goal.
- People want to achieve – so provide the conditions that help them do so.
- People have expectations that what you and your company say will take place – so don't let them down.
- People want a fair day's pay for a fair day's work – so design pay systems that assist this end.
- People want to develop – so decide what training and development is required and make sure it happens.

Conclusion

To conclude this chapter, I hope that you have found the use of a few well-chosen concepts not too academic. They have helped me to arrive at practical day-to-day means of managing people better.

They simply provide management recommendations via theoretical structures – or 'foundations'. In practice, people are complex; they have needs and values, some of which change with time and within the context of their day-to-day experience of work. Clearly, specific industries like construction form a part of the context that influences you and your people. There are obviously big differences between the everyday working environments of, say, a building site, a manufacturing plant and perhaps a doctor's surgery. However, the basic aspects of motivation do affect people's behaviour and can facilitate committed 'energy' within any organization. The end-product will always be better performance, so we should not ignore it. The clue for managers is that effective employee commitment is associated with employee satisfaction, and work satisfaction is linked to work motivational factors. Experience suggests that most activities involve employees, so it would be fair to state that managers should incorporate consideration for motivational issues as part of their daily process.

For the sake of improved performance, strive to be a good manager of people. You may find your people then view you as a leader – but don't wait for them to admit it!

Chapter **3**

Performance Management Strategies

In this chapter we look at three challenges faced by all managers who want to improve people performance:

- Have you developed an environment/working climate which encourages people to want to learn and change, adapt and improve, and eagerly look for new opportunities within your company?
- Have you the ability to get the right people in the right place with the right skills, knowledge and attitude – fast enough?
- Do you possess skills that help maintain high performance from people and, if you do, can you use those skills to retain your employees?

This chapter is written from the perspective of a middle manager of a medium-sized company in the construction industry, who wishes to ensure an appropriate climate for delivering high performance in the organization. However, sole traders, first-line managers and senior managers will also find the text useful.

Chapter 2 looked at manager and leadership attributes, style, motivation, commitment and so on. Finding the right management approach that motivates your people to perform well is clearly critical to the firm's survival and growth. However, to sustain and develop improvements in people performance you also need to think about people policies, procedures, processes such as recruitment and selection, and, crucially, to develop your own people management skills.

I start by looking at company goals, objectives and strategic plans. I then look at how communication works within the company. Attracting the right people is critical, so it is a good idea to examine the recruitment and selection process and also to consider how people are introduced to the company. I then look at how effective teams perform, giving particular attention to how they are formed and led. Teams, however, are made up of individuals; as mentioned in the previous chapter, they have different needs. They also have different problems that, from time to time, will have to be managed. To this end, a discussion of specific management skills – training, coaching, mentoring and counselling – is included. I call this the 'manager's toolbox'; these skills are not ones that will necessarily be used on an everyday basis, but they go a long way to ensuring a climate conducive to high performance. Finally, once you've got good people, how do you keep them? A high staff turnover carries cost penalties not only in finding and training new people, but also in terms of interrupting company performance. The chapter therefore ends with a discussion of staff retention strategies, paying particular attention to the role of line management in retaining good people.

Company objectives and strategic plans

For many managers, thinking about business tactics and strategy is something that is left to more senior management, the directors of the firm and the CEO (chief executive officer) or MD (managing director). However, you should have a working knowledge of this high-level process because, like it or not, you should be able to influence it, especially as your firm gets larger or you take on more management responsibilities as your career develops. Equally, most senior managers nowadays accept that it is not a good idea to divorce strategy from operational capability and will therefore need to consult with you. The most important point to remember is that policies and especially procedures and guidelines, even if high-level, influence your people and how they behave at work, so it's best you know about and engage with them.

What is strategy?

Strategy is a process whereby the organization sets its medium- to long-term aims. In essence, it means deciding where the organization is, where it wants or needs to be, and how it intends to achieve its new, preferred or best position. Even if you are a sole trader – for example, fitting kitchens, plastering, painting and decorating – you will probably have some idea about where you want your company to be in a few years' time. For larger firms in the construction industry, strategic plans and projections usually cover a medium- or long-term three- to five-year period and normally start with an external focus that includes market analysis and competitor intelligence. If you are new to this concept, Chapter 1 should have given you some idea about changes affecting the construction sector and the people who work in it that you might wish to consider. In light of this information, you would then compare competitor products and services with your own, perhaps considering issues such as the availability of your products and services, pricing and promotion.

'You have got to be careful if you don't know where you are going, because you might not get there.' (Unknown author)

As a valued colleague working in the construction business once commented, 'strategic plans might not be useful but the process of planning is crucial'. What did he mean? His experience of working in a chaotic environment had taught him that making plans for the next five years seemed like a less than good use of his time when he found it difficult to predict what would happen next month. However, in chatting with those around him, he was able to agree direction and clarify where effort could be channelled to good advantage as well as creating new ideas, medium- to long-term aspirations and agreement as to the best approach to take. The process of chatting with people was itself motivational. You may recall from the previous chapter that 'involvement' schemes and practices are important for employee self-esteem. It is the process of planning, rather than the plans themselves that helps develop cohesion and get collaboration from others. The planning process then becomes something done every year on a rolling basis and is set against company objectives (what the firm needs to attain) for the next three to five years.

You might have heard about the people element of strategic or business plans. This is called the human resource strategy. Sounds a bit high-faluting doesn't it? Chances are, however, if you work in a medium to large organization your company uses such phrases. What does it mean in 'real' language? Well, it's short-hand for that part of the overall company business strategy that is focused on people. It is essentially a people plan, providing direction against an increasing world of rapid change. Included in the strategy would be sections covering people planning (how many people with certain skills are required and where), recruitment planning (where and how will the company obtain such people), development (to what extent you can train your current people and what training new people will need) and retention (how you can hang on to your people – especially your best staff). In general terms, the HR strategy attempts to ensure that people, as a key resource of the firm, are in place and ready to meet the challenges faced by the company in establishing competitive advantage, resource capability, critical success factors and synergy. Given this long explanation of what human resource strategy means in practice, no wonder companies look for simple labels – you might even hear managers abbreviating this process and referring to HRS (human resource strategy) or strategic HRM (human resource management) issues. Critically, all managers, whatever their level within the firm, should contribute to the content of this plan, simply because you would be hard-pressed to find one manager in any medium- or large-sized firm who knows all there needs to be known about future requirements from people – so why leave it to a few strategic 'planners'? Of course, as with fully-blown business plans, there tends to be a difference or perhaps even a gulf between a five-year plan and reality. However, as indicated earlier, without any plans the company, you and your people would probably be subject to even greater turbulence.

Chapter 2 mentioned people's need for direction and recognition. To this end, they require a clearly expressed business strategy that acknowledges their importance as an essential source of added value that leads to competitive advantage. Consequently, management often include comment about their people as part of the firm's mission statement. The drafted extract shown in Figure 3.1 might provide assurance to employees that their company intends to integrate their needs.

**THE COMPANY
MISSION, VALUES AND GUIDING PRINCIPLES**

Our mission is built upon the belief in the value of our employees, our clients, our owners, and our suppliers. The business exists as a team of people. We value the effort and contribution made by each of our employees.

For our business to prevail, we must produce profit at a level to attract capital that will provide for our long-term growth and prosperity. Planning for deliberate growth will mean new opportunities for employees. Dedication to continuous improvement must be recognized. This will result in more satisfied employees, customers, expanding markets, new jobs, and will ensure company longevity.

Figure 3.1 *Extract from a draft company mission statement*

It is common for the firm's organizational mission, strategy and objectives to be informed by assessing internal strengths and weaknesses. Clearly, you would need to know how much money was available not only to fund day-to-day activities, but also to finance projects, also taking into account the use of machinery and production materials. You would also need to assess people capability. If you are a sole trader, this simply entails assessing your own capabilities, the time you have available and what you feel are the best opportunities for your business within your immediate locality. If, on the other hand, you are a manager in a small, medium or large firm, you need to assess current and planned employee skills, knowledge, attitudes, motivation and commitment to the company. Internal analysis might even record employee willingness to be flexible and responsive, their acceptance of the need to be held responsible and accountable, their enthusiasm to use their competencies for the betterment of the organization and so on. This information would be used as the initial 'employee behavioural' benchmark.

Identify the performance 'GAP'.

Managers are paid to think about growing their firm, improving performance, profits and financial returns to investors. This thought process usually reveals a gap between the company's current and desired performance. Of course, the strategy and outcomes derived from an assessment of what needs to be done (often referred to as 'gap analysis') needs to include issues related to your employees. Plans for improvement then enter the company's 'people' policies and procedures with the aim of reinforcing and sustaining the overall strategy.

As a middle manager in British Gas in the 1970s, I was very concerned about how I managed people, but was far less concerned about company policies. This was a little naive. You should remember that, as well as providing you with much-needed guidance about how to manage and implement strategy, policies and procedures provide detailed information and guidelines about the way you should manage people. They also send crucial signals to employees about the company and the way it intends to manage them. Some typical policies and procedures that are closely related to the management of people and their performance are shown in Table 3.1.

Policies	Procedures
Career management	Good salary
Employee development	Disciplinary
Employee relations	Grievances
Equal opportunities	Promotion
Health and Safety	Recruitment
Pay	Redundancy
Resourcing	Selection
Training	Transfer

Table 3.1 *Typical policies and procedures relating to people and performance management*

As can be seen from this table, policies provide a general framework for implementing people strategies whereas procedures suggest systematic managerial guidelines. There is a direct link between the day-to-day operation of personnel or human resource procedures and people's commitment to the company. The process acts as a framework through which people receive continuous information about their worth to the organization. Consequently, policies and procedures need to reinforce each other. Any apparent conflict between policies and actual managerial behaviour will result in people becoming suspicious about management intentions – certainly not an ideal situation given the link between the trust that managers have in employees (and vice versa) and high performance.

My advice is that you review your firm's policies and procedures to ensure that they provide you with adequate and appropriate guidance to manage people consistently and fairly. Another thing that is sometimes forgotten with regard to plans and policies is that their content should help you engage with your people. You may recall from Chapter 2 that people have certain work needs and motivation. A quick look at the policies listed in Table 3.1 confirms the linkage between motivation and company policy. Some examples might be a person's motivational need for security and policies such as health and safety and pay, or a person's need for self-esteem and policies such as employee development and training, or an employee's need to achieve and policies such as career development and procedures such as appraisal and promotion. I hope I have made my point.

As a manager, you can also use policies and procedures incorrectly. From experience, let me have a humorous stab at what I mean.

*If you want plans, policies and procedures to **fail**:*

Stage 1   Ensure that the content of strategic plans is developed by people who are disengaged from operational or market-related reality.

Stage 2   Base the plan on assumptions that few below the author(s) of the plan would recognize and/or endorse its content.

Stage 3   Keep most people in the dark. Senior managers should not discuss underlying assumptions or implications with middle and/or first-line managerial staff. After all, plans are normally only written to satisfy the needs of those above, and discussion only attracts too many opinions that might obscure simplicity.

Stage 4   Make sure that the plans contain impossible, or at least unrealistic, targets so that, even if others find out about the plan, they cannot be motivated.

Stage 5   Avoid any attempt to subject plans to risk analysis. But if it must be done, ensure that key interventions aimed at managing risk remain on paper only.

Stage 6   Make sure that the plans are not supported by appropriate policies and that those policies and procedures cause confusion.

Stage 7   In one year's time, go back to stage 1.

Strategic planning, policy formulation and the issue of procedures and work practices do two things. They communicate direction and they indicate how the company should use its resources – money, materials, time, space and people. Your responsibility is to communicate and use their content to help you improve people performance.

Communication: What a manager needs to know

The need for appropriate communication is also associated with employee commitment. Consider job-related information for example. The 1981 CBI Workplace Industrial Relations Survey found that the industrial climate was more favourably assessed by both trade unions and the workforce as a whole when management gave a lot of information to employees. It also reported a high correlation between those employees regarding themselves as well informed and those reporting a high degree of job satisfaction.

A major survey conducted by the Institute of Directors in 1991, involving 115 medium and large companies in Britain (including some from the construction industry) found that extra attention from management on the need to communicate gave rise to a range of improvements (see Table 3.2).

Activity	% Improvement
Improved morale/commitment	80
Fewer industrial disputes	68
Increased productivity	65
Better customer relations	47
Reduced employee turnover	46
Less time lost through absenteeism	41
Difficult to evaluate	8
No improvements	3
	[n = 115]

Source: Institute of Directors (1991).

Table 3.2 *Improvements attributed to communication initiatives*

It is true that most managers I speak with say that communication is something they or their firm never get quite right. They often use the word 'something' because the subject is so broad and complex that it is difficult to pin down, but I will try.

Plans and procedures should be good enough to communicate important issues to employees on our behalf. However, I think that we managers also communicate in everything we say, write, do, express, act, decide, show, move or gesture. Consequently, when I talk about appraisals, training, and performance measures and so on, they all involve a process of communication, so, best to start off with a few obvious areas.

Formal communication

Communication: formal, informal, upward, downward and across.

First, the formal communication process in companies involves what management want to say and may be based on what management think employees need to know. Clearly, senior managers will want employees to take on the values of the firm. For example, you will want employees to know about plans, intentions or proposals, especially if they are invited, or expected, to comment on them. You will also want to clearly state the company's objectives, policies, project plans, budget information and so on to those who need to know them, and more directly communicate 'work activity' instructions, performance measures and results to everyone and every team. Often overlooked but equally important, you may also want your people to communicate upwards and provide innovative ideas and/or suggest how work can be more efficiently organized, and perhaps also obtain information about levels of employee satisfaction. To this end, you, as manager, may use common communication devices such as company bulletins, magazines, newsletters, noticeboards, videos, CDs, team briefings, quality improvement meetings, innovation boxes, appraisals, employee surveys, coaching, training, suggestion schemes and so on. Local building firms that I have worked with report that communication devices involving one-to-one dialogue seem to provide the most current and usable information. This approach seems particularly useful when we realize that the construction industry needs to innovate. As mentioned in Chapter 1, innovation rests on the manager's ability to capture and use individual expertise and creative thinking skills in order to create or apply new knowledge from inside the organization.

Then there is the matter of what your people want to hear. Clearly, your people will be interested in anything that affects their interests, needs and motivation. Obvious items requiring communication would include site or office working conditions, job security, new work practices, potential changes to your people's conditions of employment, pay, overtime arrangements, holidays, shiftworking patterns and, as mentioned earlier, company plans that may affect all the other items. Your job is to not only communicate essential information, but also to listen to what your people say and act appropriately.

It becomes obvious, when you begin to list what managers and employees want to say and hear, that, despite clear similarities, there are some differences. Hence the occasional occurrence of communication problems and disputes. This is an area discussed in Chapter 4. Here, I will just say that, in my opinion, communication only takes place when the receiver of the communication acts on the information given – hopefully, in accordance with the sender's wishes.

The construction industry's dynamic working environment is not always beneficial to good communication. The sheer number of different jobs or activities involved suggests that communication will always be difficult. For example, people working in trowel occupations, woodworking occupations, construction and civil engineering, interior systems, roof slating, steel-fixing, insulation, rigging and demolition will have different responsibilities, tasks, schedules, reporting systems and so on. So, if your people have been told something, never assume that the rest of the firm will have the same information, that the person or group understood it in the first place, and that the person or group will remember what you said for ever.

It is best to accept that there are barriers to communication – obstacles that get in the way of a communication being heard, being interpreted correctly or being received. For example, you may not have understood the message given to you, you may not express your thoughts adequately, there may be too many distractions preventing the communication from being received, the receiver may not want to listen and so on. It all adds up to the old conundrum: 'I know what I thought I said, you know what you think you heard me say, I think you understood what I thought I had said, you think I understand what you thought you heard me say.' Fortunately, you can do something about most barriers – if you are aware of them. The most obvious solution is to ask questions and watch out for signs of confusion – for example, puzzled or frustrated looks, people asking other members of the group questions, or simply resistance.

Interpersonal skills

It may also be obvious to you that communication involves your ability to exercise your interpersonal skills. Although the Institute of Directors survey is impressive, improvements are not necessarily a reaction to improved communication. Improvements in performance also occurred because management showed a willingness to communicate with employees. Do you like people to talk *with you* or talk *at you*? Whilst not denying the importance of communicating factual and results-related information, what appears to be of equal importance is the process of communicating – how you go about communicating in your workplace. It is a large part of your job and it involves working with and through others. The application of effective interpersonal skills is an important tool for removing most communication barriers. Put simply, in my experience, interpersonal skills make the difference between success and failure. A lack of skill on your part will impede your people's performance. The following self-assessment questionnaire lists some important management skills; try self-assessing yourself by rating your current performance on each using a scale of 1 to 5.

Self-assessment Questionnaire: Communication Skills

- Developing and maintaining rapport
  with your people and more senior management [   ]
- Listening to others [   ]
- Asking relevant questions [   ]
- Showing sensitivity to others [   ]
- Getting ideas and making sure they are
  considered by the right people at the right time [   ]
- Getting a feel about what your people think
  about changes and, if appropriate, making sure
  more senior management know about them [   ]
- Influencing others [   ]
- Problem- and conflict-solving [   ]
- Knowing how to handle the information given
  to you to communicate up, down and across
  your company [   ]
- Knowing how to work under pressure and
  manage stress [   ]
- Acting assertively, not aggressively or
  non-assertively [   ]

I have chosen a few of the above areas for further explanation.

Assertive behaviour

First, what is the difference between passive, aggressive and assertive management behaviour?

Passive behaviour might include:

- putting yourself down
- accepting being put down by others
- comparing yourself unfavourably with others
- having unrealistic targets that are doomed to failure
- reminding yourself about past failures
- being too self-critical.

Aggressive behaviour might be shown by:

- thinking that you are always right and your people are always wrong – after all, you are the boss
- always needing to win arguments
- thinking that it does not matter if you hurt people as long as you get your own way
- demanding that other people must change – not you
- always wanting to be in command.

I have noticed that aggressive managers tend to stare, look down on people, speak loudly or speak quietly but menacingly (perhaps the worst form), point their finger and/or hammer the table and talk over other people, stopping them in their tracks. They also tend to take a physical position of dominance and control, folding their arms and showing anger or disbelief, displeasure and perhaps nervousness. Do you know anyone like this?

Assertive behaviour is usually the best option. It involves adopting the following attitudes:

- All have important views and contributions to make.
- Involving people is generally a good idea – although, of course, there are limits to involvement when critical deadlines are approaching.
- I have rights, but so do you.

Assertive behaviour that I observe and want to imitate includes calmness, confidence, contentment and a powerful, fair but firm demeanour.

Stress

I realize that it is all very well for me to suggest behaving assertively but how can you do it when you are stressed from overwork, tight deadlines and too little time – common problems in the construction industry? There are no easy answers – just a few comments and suggestions. Start by writing down the five most important causes or contributions to your feeling stressed at work on the chart below.

Stress Assessment Chart

Stressor (Note the form of work stress, i.e. poor manager, overwork, time)	Rating (How severe is it? Use a scale of 1–10)	Reason (Why do you think it occurs?)
1		
2		
3		
4		
5		

If you are experiencing stress, then you are probably not performing as well as you should. Also, remember that if your people are stressed they won't be highly effective either. Stress is a very expensive cost to UK industry – in excess of £3 billion a year. Typical and increasingly common symptoms include alcoholism, drugs, absenteeism, premature death and early retirement.

In simple terms, stress is anything that leads to a person experiencing stress, which is perhaps best termed as feelings of distress. Common stressors include:

- interpersonal conflict
- bereavement
- doing presentations
- heights
- answering the telephone.

You might notice that this is a peculiar list. I chose it in order to point out that distress is an individual thing. Being stressed by answering the telephone is probably something few of us suffer from. Nevertheless, to those who do, it can be devastating. Categories of stress might include:

- *Change*. Change is not always something welcomed by everyone, and too much too quickly will stress most people.
- *Too many demands*. I'm sure you know what this one feels like, so no further comment is necessary.

- *Insufficient stimulation.* Believe it or not, many people suffer badly from boredom.
- *Worries, fears and phobias.* Think about how family concerns affect your work performance, or how an economic downturn can threaten jobs, or a bricklayer who suddenly gets a fear of heights or people who are worried about their health or their job, or who have money problems.

Others might include poor communication, too little to do, too many difficult things to accomplish, and not enough experience, training or management support. Communication (or the lack of it) can be a stressor in the following ways:

- People don't tell me things I should know.
- I don't tell others things they should know.
- I don't admit things to myself.

And worst of all:

- I'm not clear what I'm supposed to be doing.

As a manager you may also want to know if any of your people feel like a square peg in a round hole. I have managed many people who fit this problem. They are working in a group of people who reject them, or doing a job that they are over- or under-qualified to do, or have simply outgrown their current job and are ready for additional responsibility and authority. Whatever the reason, they have stopped performing well and may show signs of being stressed – it is your job to find out why. You can do this by using coaching and/or counselling techniques (described later on in this chapter).

Recognize your limitations!

Be aware that there are many causes of stress, including medical ones – in which case recognize your limitations and urge the person concerned to seek professional advice. However, as stress can affect work behaviour and hence performance, it is likely that you, as their manager, will be the first to spot work problems. Look for signs that indicate that you or your people:

- have trouble concentrating
- show difficulty making decisions
- have trouble in remembering things
- find it difficult to 'turn off'
- day-dream excessively
- tend to lose their temper
- demonstrate poor judgement
- take longer over tasks
- make more errors
- unusually and unnecessarily double-check everything they do
- are absent more than usual over long periods
- are unusually late or seem unusually lethargic.

Clearly, a cluster of behavioural signs is usually a more reliable indicator than a single sign that a member of staff may be experiencing undue levels of stress.

Some common ways of reducing stress levels include:

- exercise
- yoga
- meditation
- relaxation therapy
- going for a walk – take the dog
- taking up a new hobby
- speaking to someone you trust – a problem shared is a problem halved
- recognizing your rights – try being more assertive, less passive and/or less aggressive
- improving your time management
- delegating
- understanding the nature of conflict.

Poor communication can be a cause of stress – at either the receiving or giving end.

Communicating to groups

Managers in the construction industry may experience problems with communication because they are often distanced from many of their employees and some of their managers, hence the need to use several communication devices previously mentioned. The other reason is that, quite simply, they are short of time.

To save time, you can communicate with many or all of your people at the same time. This has the advantage that each one of your people hears the same thing, your communication is direct and you get (or may get) immediate feedback – their views. However, if you make a mistake in front of your people then it may take a long time to 'live it down', so here are a few pointers.

Decide what you are going to tell your group. Write down the topic you are going to talk about. If you are going to talk about several related topics, write down one sentence for each. Then write down your objectives, what you want your people to do, future action, what needs to achieved and so on. Finally, note down what you are going to say – sometimes one word for each point is sufficient. Remember to:

1 put your notes into a logical sequence
2 write down in full all important questions which require answers/opinions
3 underline important points.

You are not giving a training session (training techniques are covered more fully in Chapter 4), although you might divide up your notes in the following manner:

1 *Introduction.* State the purpose of the group meeting.
2 *Main body.* Make each point step-by-step. It you are going to talk for more than ten minutes, make sure you summarize important points frequently.
3 *Conclusion.* Ask for, and definitely answer, questions (even if the answer is 'I don't know, but I will find out and get back to you'). Then summarize (once again) the main points, especially those that require action and results from the group.

Then select an appropriate communication method. There are three common methods:

1 *The straight talk.* This is the best method to use when you are giving a set of instructions that are straightforward and must be followed.
2 *Questions and answers.* This is the best method to use when you want to get your people's views and opinions or test reactions to a new activity or process.
3 *The discussion.* Use this method when you want to involve other people or stimulate new ideas. It is similar to the question-and-answer method except that your people will usually talk with each other, as well as to you.

Generally, try to use the right method for the right purpose. I know this is obvious, but it is important. For example, if you want to find out why your team are taking longer to complete a job in comparison with other teams, you will have to raise the issue and then ask lots of questions. It is unlikely that a droning monologue about being more efficient will have a significant effect on performance – try to engage the interest of your people.

Essential to good communication with a group of your people is selecting the right environment – it will influence the behaviour of the people you talk to. Ask yourself the following questions:

1 Should I use my office or a site office? Is it big enough? What about interruptions?
2 Should I use their office (if they share work space)? Again is it big enough? Is it private enough? Will we be overheard?
3 Can we use somewhere else – for example, a conference room, someone else's facilities or a canteen? Is it suitable for what I will be saying or asking questions about? Will it be noisy?
4 Will I be seated or will I stand? Will I stand and my people sit? Remember, they must be able to hear you and, for most situations, you must not take a position that may appear overdomineering.
5 Will I talk from behind a desk or with no barriers between me and my group? On a general note, it is best to remove barriers.

6   Will we all sit round a table? This can be useful, especially for open discussion and when documents, reports or files are to be issued.

If you need some visual aids such as paper, pencils, handouts, flipcharts, computer(s), screen, projector and so on, make sure that the equipment is ready and working before your people come into the room. Fiddling around while people watch in a deathly silence is not a good start – especially if you are going to talk about the need for more efficient and effective operations!

When the meeting is finished, try asking yourself a few basic questions. Did my people understand what they must do? Did I leave them reasonably enthused? If the answer is 'yes' to both, give yourself a pat on the back. Finally, ask yourself: 'Do I need to take any further action?'

You may be thinking that the above guidelines are far too complicated for a simple chat with a group of people. Ask yourself how well you currently communicate in groups? If the answer is 'I never have problems and what I say is always understood', then I agree that the above guidelines may be overstated. If you have experienced problems communicating with groups of people, try the above process – the more you try it, the more it will become second nature.

Making communication more time-efficient

Here are a few other pointers about how to manage your time well:

1   Avoid time-wasters, such as incomplete information, being kept waiting, lack of training, being unsure of your priorities, poor communication, management by crisis and making mistakes. Meet people in their office or environment – it is much easier to walk away. Prepare polite excuses to shorten conversations or visits. If you get an unplanned visitor, try to remain standing until you know whether a discussion is required. You may find that you have to make yourself inaccessible at particular times – close your door (if you have one) or try to find a private location where you can think.
2   Insist that people attending meetings arrive on time and make sure the agenda concerns all who attend. Prepare the agenda carefully and send it out well before the meeting. Keep meetings disciplined and moving forward. For example, follow the agenda and discourage less relevant side issues. Finish meetings on time.
3   When taking telephone calls, ask the caller specifically how you can help. Make sure you have the information you need near at hand and prepare polite excuses to shorten the call. Use e-mail whenever possible – but remember not to forget the value of that 'personal touch'.

'It has become appallingly obvious that our technology has exceeded out humanity.'
(Albert Einstein)

Improving written communication

'I'm all in favour of keeping dangerous weapons out of the hands of fools. Let's start with typewriters.' (Frank Lloyd Wright)

Of course, communication essentially involves both verbal and written skills. I have included some ideas about verbal skills as part of the manager as trainer section in Chapter 4. As for written skills, here are a few basic ideas that I try to adopt and which you might find interesting.

When writing e-mails, memorandums or letters try the following golden rules. As you go through each rule, self-assess your current performance. Ask yourself whether each rule is something you do well or is something you could improve on:

- Decide the purpose of your written communication.
- Think through the background and experience of those who will receive your document.
- Remember that you are trying to get and hold their attention.
- State clearly the purpose for writing – for example, 'I am writing to express my concern over the amount of overtime …' or 'I am writing to let you know that …'.
- Sort through the information you need to include in the document. Try to put it into a logical order.
- Use short simple sentences whenever possible.
- Shorten phrases – try to be concise without losing the meaning of what you want to communicate.
- Avoid repetition – if you bore the reader they are unlikely to remember what you said or intended to convey. Of course, they may remember that you bored them!
- Use a paragraph for each step. Make sure that connected ideas come together in one main theme – different themes need separate paragraphs.
- Try to lead in and from each paragraph – for instance, 'It is important I mention this because …'.
- Avoid too much technical or business jargon. If you have to use it, make sure that the word you use is not open to a different interpretation.
- Correct spelling errors – same-sounding words can have totally different meanings.
- Pay attention to punctuation – it can change the meaning of what you intended to say.
- Evaluate the tone of the communication and remember who will be reading it – people often sound too harsh when writing.
- Remember that communicating in writing is different from talking and that you use different words from those you use in conversation. Stick to the point; avoid information that gets in the way of what you are trying to say.
- End by pointing the way ahead – what you want the reader to do and/or what you want the reader to expect to happen.

I have sometimes found it useful, when expressing my opinion about something in writing, to invite the reader to comment. Also remember that one important advantage that writing has over talking is that writing provides a permanent record of the request, your views, your concerns, your advice and so on.

Informal communication

Communication should not be limited to formal with your people if you want to benefit from new ideas, important or unexpected information or simply spot early warning signs of trouble. Daily contact, perhaps best described or known as 'the one-minute manager' technique, simply suggests that you should try to find one minute for a brief chat with as many of your people as possible. Formal meetings should assist communication, direction, promote discussion and so on. However, outside of meetings, it is amazing how much information you can give and receive in one minute on an informal basis. Make use of those unplanned encounters on site, in corridors, in the car park and so on. The informality of such meetings helps people relax and discuss issues that might be left unsaid in other settings. In my experience, such contact provides you with essential information about real concerns and blockages that get in the way of performance improvements.

You may also have heard of 'walking-the-floor' and 'back-to-the-floor' activities. These are activities usually considered by more senior managers in larger firms. Nevertheless, they can have very positive effects if used by middle management. Simply, they are ways that you might infrequently visit work areas/sites and show interest, speaking *with* people (not *at* people). The back-to-the-floor concept involves you in doing work you don't have to do. Laying a few bricks in winter or taking a few customer calls and having a chat with people while on the job can provide valuable information, and this type of contact is usually well received by employees.

Of course, contact with your people does not have to be a daily occurrence or always of a personal nature. If you are physically disconnected from contact, you need to make more use of devices such as noticeboards and e-mail. It is also worth noting the existence of the 'grapevine'. This is the well-known, but very informal, communication process that people use in most firms to circulate pieces of information, gossip or insider facts or opinions outside formal communication systems. As a manager, you need to know what the grapevine is saying – especially when unfounded and potentially damaging rumours occur that you need to suppress. However, you can also use the process to your own advantage. For example, a well-meaning management response to an employee in difficulty spreads through the organization like wildfire. I am not suggesting you use manipulative 'mind games', simply that good as well as bad news in most firms is circulated by means of the very informal grapevine communication process. A little good news can really help performance.

'A lie gets halfway around the world before the truth has a chance to get its pants on.' (Sir Winston Churchill)

One successful idea put into practice by a 'blue-chip' multi-national organization was to offer all employees the chance to e-mail the managing director with problems and frustrations, ideas, personal and/or group views and so on. The initiative opened up direct communication where previous direct contact had either not existed or communication had become filtered to such a degree that the original message had become blurred. Initially, employees were suspicious that 'the boss' was not in fact the person responding to their e-mails, then they were amazed that communication could be so candid. The managing director's reputation as someone who recognized the importance of employee opinion grew almost overnight. The managing director was equally impressed with the quality of contact. In this technological age such an idea should not be limited to contact with senior management.

Asking questions and giving feedback

As you go through the rest of this chapter you will notice that the need to understand and use questioning techniques effectively is a critical part of the manager's toolkit. This is not as obvious as it sounds. To help you, here are a few guidelines about the type of questions you can use:

1 *Open questions*. These usually start with open words such as 'What', 'How' and 'Why'. Use them to get more detail – for example, about a candidate's work experience, knowledge or skills.
2 *Searching questions*. These usually start with words such as 'Who', 'When' and 'Where'. Use them when you are seeking specific information.
3 *Closed questions*. These can be used to clarify a point – they receive yes/no answers. Use wording such as 'Have you …?', 'Do you …?', 'Will you …?', 'Could you …?', 'Would you …?' and 'Haven't you …?'.
4 *Agreement seekers*. These are similar to closed questions: 'It's a fine day isn't it?' 'Do you agree with the responsibilities of your job?'.
5 *Amplifying questions*. If you do not get a sufficiently open answer to one of your open questions try using an amplifying question such as 'Tell me more', 'Can you explain further?' 'Can you describe?'.

Adopting the right form of question at the right time is a crucial management skill. My advice is to make a conscious effort to try wording your questions differently and see how they affect the information you receive. Many managers concentrate on questions that get a yes or no answer. You may be interested to know that most people prefer getting open questions such as 'What do you think of …?'. Clearly, such questions suggest to the receiver that you care about their opinion – in many ways, open questions are a form of recognition (the crucial motivation discussed in Chapter 2).

For me, this view was recently confirmed when working with several metropolitan borough council housing departments. It was agreed that, during particularly intense periods of change, questions that promoted greater discussion led to improved understanding. Nevertheless, all forms of question have their place: the art (or skill) is asking the right form at the right time.

As well as making sure you receive adequate information, you also have to know how to give it – this is called giving feedback. Feedback is simply a means by which you give information to others about how they have done, or are currently doing, their job and how they affect other people. Similarly, you can attract and receive feedback (information) about your own impact on people – always useful. Asking staff open questions about how they think your section, department or project team is doing and what could be done to improve performance usually prompts useful comment.

If people are performing badly you must not ignore it. From experience, the poor performance does not go away – it usually gets worse. As a manager, you have to provide feedback. If you do it well, it can help motivate your people. In many respects, it is a further form of recognition.

Obviously, when giving feedback you must make sure that it is done in such a way that it does not end in people performing badly. So here are a few of my golden rules:

- Give feedback as close to the event that triggered it.
- Before giving feedback examine your own motivation. Why do you need to give feedback, what is your reason and what do you want the result to look like?
- Give feedback that is focused on behaviour, not the person. Comment on what you observed. Avoid comments like 'What you did was …' and 'What your problem is …'. Refer to 'I' rather than 'you'. For example:
  - 'I have noticed that some people seem very anxious after attending appraisal – am I right to think that?'
  - 'I sometimes get cost reports that suggest control could be improved – what do you think?'
  - 'I am concerned that too many people are absent or late on Monday mornings – should I be?'
- Be specific about the information you need to give – don't ramble.
- Observe the impact of your words and then listen to what the other person has to say.
- Don't sit in judgement. If the information you need to give is negative, you are trying to communicate that, but also get agreement for the need for change.
- Remember, feedback can be positive. Praise when and where it is due is a powerful way of increasing people's motivation. The general rule is to give more positive than negative feedback. I have found that, even in the worse situations, you

can say something positive even if, on balance, the feedback given is negative. If you are always negative, you risk being ignored and disrespected. Unfortunately, disrespect is difficult to combat; once disrespected, you may only have one other course of action – that is, to employ the company disciplinary procedure. Of course, when you have to rely on the authority of the firm to take over responsibility, that is the stage at which you may have failed as a manager.

- Remember, what you say is your opinion – the other person is not necessarily wrong. You simply have a right to say what you feel. They, of course, have a right to reject your view.
- Try to work toward joint understanding.
- Follow up feedback by offering constructive ideas on how to improve performance.

Sometimes your people may be reluctant to talk with you, or they may not be concise. There will also be many occasions when you need to drag relevant information or ideas out of people – perhaps in order to resolve conflicts. The skill required here is called 'effective questioning'. Generally, use open, searching and amplifying questions. You may also find a counselling approach useful. More information about this vital manager skill is given in 'The manager's toolbox of skills' later in this chapter.

Finally, I recall a few ideas that have made a big impact on me and, hopefully, on the way I communicate and manage others. Although basic, they are ideas that are frequently forgotten, especially while we are trying to get to grips with everyday workloads and work problems. Here they are:

- Talk 'up to people', not 'down to them'.
- Despite problems and pressures, stay positive.
- Give your people more warm comments than cold ones.
- Manage and lead by example.
- Remember that recognition works wonders.
- Be straight with people.
- When communicating changes seek out and emphasize incentives.
- It is human to make a mistake – just emphasize that mistakes should not be repeated.
- Of course, some mistakes can be so devastating that making them threatens life itself. For these, you need to ensure people are highly trained to avoid them and are well aware of the possible consequences.
- Managing is all about maintaining a healthy balance between extremes. More is said about this in Chapter 5.

'A doctor can bury his mistakes but an architect can only advise his clients to plant vines.'
(Frank Lloyd Wright)

Recruiting and selecting people

The government-backed Rethinking Construction M41 working group has been working to achieve high-level support from the most forward-thinking construction companies. They comment that the construction industry is in competition for the best people and must commit itself to achieving significantly sustained improvement in performance if it is to recruit, retain and get the best from its people. Excellent company performance attracts good people and helps retain them. It is also true that people performance relates to the way we recruit, retain, develop and manage employees. As for recruitment and selection, Walt Disney offers his view: 'We are looking for personality. We want people who are enthusiastic, who have pride in their work, who can take charge of a situation without supervision.' You may recall the details given in Chapter 2 about the kind of commitment managers want from people – the word 'enthusiastic' seems all-important and is critical to obtaining high performance.

Uncle Walt's comment seems valid if, as managers, we are presented with a 'greenfield' opportunity to personally oversee the recruitment of all our staff in one go. Clearly, this is not always the case. Gaining enthusiasm is not so easy when we have to inherit employees and want them to perform better, especially if they are remembering previous negative work experiences that may prevent improvements in their personal performance. Even if we were able to pick our own staff, are we really able to identify the right personality, skills and knowledge? I have known managers decide on a candidate's suitability based on the design of their tie. Nevertheless, the best way of making sure that the organization benefits from high-performing employees is to recruit and select the right people in the first place: the right people at the right time in the right place with the right knowledge and skills and the willingness to apply their energies for the betterment of the organization's goals – a tall order indeed.

It is important to mention some key steps that a manager may take. Too often, managers turn to specialist recruitment staff to recruit employees for them. In my experience, many line managers and supervisors believe that their role in recruitment and selection should end with a request to personnel to employ some more staff and to give some vague idea as to the job itself. Given the obvious truth that it may cost the firm over £40 000 to recruit an employee and even more to get rid of that person should they prove unsuitable, taking time out in an attempt to recruit the right person for the job is usually well rewarded. It is a manager activity that can boost productivity and hence bottom-line profit, it can save managerial time, reduce the real cost of recruitment and avoid considerable strain on the manager's own patience and/or stress levels. So what can the manager do? There are some key steps and guidelines to recruitment and selection.

First, decide on requirements. These are job-related; refer to the job description and personal specification. You need a list of requirements – for example:

- the overall purpose of the job
- the main tasks/accountabilities
- details as to overall responsibility
- key result areas
- performance standards
- who the employee will report to
- special requirements, such as use of tools and equipment
- other features, such as shift- or nightwork, a need to work in different environments, specific working conditions and so on.

A person specification would also include:

- qualifications
- specific skills
- work-based and behavioural competencies – for example, 'You must be able to communicate effectively both verbally and in writing'.

If you are a sole trader or small enterprise wishing to take on a few new people, you may wish to use the basic job and person specifications depicted in Figures 3.2 and 3.3.

You then need to think about attracting candidates. Consider whether preference will (or can) be given to internal candidates. What will the effect be on current employees if you advertise externally but not internally? What media will you use? It must be an appropriate media. Think about:

- using the popular press, or quality papers
- advertising in suitable journals – for instance, managerial, professional, construction industry/trade and/or technical journals
- approaching a recruitment agency
- hiring recruitment or executive search consultants
- contacting and working with further or higher educational establishments.

Job Specification	
Department:	Section/Project team:
Job title:	Job grade:
Reporting to (job title):	
Responsible for (job titles):	
Overall purpose of job:	
Main duties/activities/tasks *(List each activity/task and categorize as desirable (D) or essential (E))*	
Special requirements *(tools and equipment used, external contacts, etc.)*	
Other features of the job *(shift- or nightwork, travel, working conditions, etc.)*	
Location of job:	

Figure 3.2 *Sample job specification form*

Person Specification
Education, qualifications and special training (if required):
Experience:
Work-based competencies (knowledge and skills):

Essential	Desirable

Behavioural competencies (applications):

Essential	Desirable

Figure 3.3 *Sample person specification form*

When advertising, it will be necessary to provide an advertisement that attracts attention. If you are writing or designing the advertisement, follow the guidelines below:

1 Have a relevant and attractive headline.
2 Quote the salary/wage.
3 Display the name of your firm.
4 Create interest in the position, but do not oversell. There is little point overstating the position as you will only attract people who will reject the job at the interview stage or, worse still, resign after a short period of service when they find the job was not what they envisaged.
5 Add further information that might attract appropriate candidates – for example, career prospects, pension arrangements, a statement about your equal opportunities policy and so on.
6 Mention the qualifications, experience and personal qualities that are required.
7 End the advertisement stating how the candidate should apply and when – perhaps giving a closing date for applications.

Sift through the applications. This is a task that many managers find laborious. My only advice is to concentrate on what the candidates say and how they sell themselves. I usually make two pre-lists that state:

1 what a candidate must be able to do and how they must behave
2 what a candidate should be able to do and how they should behave.

Compare all the applications with your key criteria which emanate from the job description and personal specification. Check your 'must' and 'should' list; then, based on the information given by the candidate, prepare a shortlist for inclusion in the selection process. I always find it useful to work with one or two other people and ask them also to prepare their 'must' and 'should' lists and their shortlist for selection. In terms of the shortlisting and selection process, two minds are always better than one.

You now need to think about how you will select new employees. In many ways, the information you will receive will relate to what you are willing to spend in order to retrieve it. Clearly, the type of job and the wage/salary of the job have a big impact as to what selection method/s you will choose. You and your selection panel can use one or several selection techniques. The most common of these are described below.

Interviews

Interviews are generally the most common form of selection. They ensure that you come face-to-face with each of the shortlisted candidates for the job. Using one interviewer might attract bias, but using two or three interviewers allows you to discuss the relevant merits of each candidate and check each other for possible bias. The aim of the interview is to provide answers to important questions. For example, does the candidate fit the job and personal specification and, more simply, can and will the candidate be able to do the job? How will the individual fit into the proposed team, section, site, organization and so on?

As for interview techniques, try applying the following:

1 Prepare and plan for the interview. Organize a room in advance and decide on timing. Make notes and list questions that cover the specific areas you wish to discuss. If necessary, list a few closed questions to help steer the interview, but then concentrate on using open questions. If there is more than one interviewer make sure that you each ask relevant questions and that they do not overlap – unless it is a critical area which you wish the panel to probe.

2 At the start of the interview make the candidate feel at ease. You are unlikely to get desired information if the candidate is tense and guarded. So, do not start your questioning with a question that is demanding and difficult to answer. Encourage the candidate to talk. A good interview is one in which the candidate does 80 per cent of the talking.

3 During the interview concentrate on what you need to know. Probe where necessary. Make sure you cover all the key areas – don't allow a candidate to leave without having received an answer to crucial questions that relate to important areas of the job.

Non-verbal communication is behaviour and bodily gestures that act as messages about what someone is thinking.

4 Try to analyse behaviour. This is difficult but crucial. Remember, you want a person who not only *can do the job*, but also *will do the job*. Sometimes, open questions about a candidate's career or interests can reveal patterns of behaviour. Watching out for tell-tale non-verbal communication can be of assistance, but make sure you receive some training before you put too much trust in your perceptions of non-verbal cues.

5 Maintain control. You may have already experienced an interview where the candidate seemed to be interviewing the interviewer or where the candidate simply talked about issues or events that showed them in a good light. I have witnessed interviews where it was established that the candidate and interviewer had a shared interest in the same football team and where the dialogue never seemed to drift toward actual job requirements. Don't allow candidates to gloss over important job requirements.

6 Don't jump to conclusions. There is a tendency in interviews to make a decision about candidates too early – first impressions *can* be wrong.

Using interviews is advantageous because they involve face-to-face dialogue. They can provide the interviewer and the candidate with an opportunity to gauge whether they would fit the job and the organization. For instance, you will know what the specific construction-related working environment entails and at least some of the characters the new employee would need to work with – will they be able to fit in? Equally, to the candidate, you, as interviewer, are an ambassador of your organization, so they will be eager to find out as much from you as they can about what it would be like to work for you and work in the company.

There are, however, some potential disadvantages of using interviews – namely:

- Interviewers must be highly skilled to use the process well.
- For many jobs in the construction industry, they do not directly test actual skills/individual competencies.
- They can lead to bias and poor judgements about a candidate's suitability.
- They are not always a good means of predicting performance and, preferably, other selection methods should be used to supplement and to check out key areas of the job candidate's abilities and characteristics.

Selection tests

Selection tests range from practical demonstration, intelligence tests to examine numerical and verbal reasoning to self-report personality tests. Some detail may assist:

Psychometric tests

Psychometric tests use sets of questions – for example, numerical/mathematical questions – that require answers within a set time. Answers are then measured against a significant number of other people's answers to the same questions. The candidate's score can then be seen within a normal distribution curve. The result shows each candidate's score against other candidates – or a total population. It would indicate whether a candidate has an average, an above-average, or below-average score as compared with others in the same industry or profession. Some larger organizations also have their own data by which to compare candidates.

Personality tests

Personality tests provide self-report answers to behavioural questions. Questions are grouped into clusters that purport to measure personality traits such as decisiveness, competitiveness, caring, anxiety, personal energy and so on. There are also questionnaires that provide details of suitable careers or measures of commitment and/or motivations. Several reputable 'instruments' are available, although some are costly and most require expert training to administer. Nevertheless, in my view, the results they provide constitute acceptable information that helps in making a decision about a candidate. However, I would not use these instruments or take heed of their results without additional evidence. A combination of methods is always desirable.

Practical demonstration

Practical demonstration is the best form of evidence as to whether a candidate can do the job. If you are recruiting a bricklayer, ask them to lay a few bricks within a given time to a given quality standard. If secretarial duties require typing skills, then ask the candidate to do some typing and check for errors.

Assessment centres

Assessment centres seem costly – but are they really in the longer term?

Assessment centres are not a place; they are an event. They are particularly useful as a focus on behaviour. To some extent, they can examine a person's willingness, as well as their ability, to do the job. They may incorporate an interview and tests. However, they also provide exercises that are specifically designed to simulate key dimensions of the job. For example, team leadership might involve role-plays, site managers might be required to sift through an in-tray, project team members may be required to take part in a group discussion and so on. Importantly, throughout the assessment centre event, performance is measured by a number of observers. This idea raises the objectivity level of the selection process. For example, several candidates can be assessed together to provide observers with information about how each candidate interacts with others and participates in, or contributes to, the discussion. However, assessment centres can be costly, they take up a lot of management time, assessor observers must be trained before the event and, if psychometric tests are used, you need expert advice. Nevertheless, a well-constructed and delivered assessment centre can achieve a better forecast of a potential employee's actual work performance.

Assessment centres are also used for developing existing staff and for career planning purposes. I use this method to discover competencies in people that are seen as critical to the future success of the business. For example, when a housing department of a local authority becomes a private sector-financed housing trust, certain competencies change. Assessment centres provide observers with evidence of actual behaviour in new situations as well as reviewing specific numerical and verbal reasoning abilities.

The final stage

Finally, you and your selection panel will pick the best person(s) for the job(s). You will need to contact the successful candidates and break the good news. I like to do this myself initially over the phone; it shows interest in people and it is always useful to listen to the candidate's reaction. Follow up with a letter confirming the appointment and arrange a convenient start date and time.

How to introduce people to the company

Can you remember your first day at your new company? Or perhaps you have had many? If so, you will realize that the way you are treated has a big impact on you. However mature you are, your first moments in a new work environment are likely to have a lasting effect – one that will impact on your overall commitment to the organization. How good is your company induction?

The aim of the induction process is to help ensure that the new employee starts with a favourable attitude towards the company. After all, they will be spending a third of their daily life there. From a business-only perspective, a person who has received an appropriate introduction to the firm is more likely to become a fully effective worker in the shortest possible time and therefore stay with the firm, so here are a few ideas to make the first moments a good experience for both you and the new employee:

First impressions last.

1 Greet the person on arrival. If the new employee is reporting to a reception area, leave word with reception to expect them.
2 The employee should then be greeted by a person in authority who will provide basic information about the company and the new employee's terms and conditions as well as being able to explain any employment-related issues. A standard set of important items is as follows:
   - hours of work, holidays, lunch periods, sickness notification
   - pension, pay, union arrangements, training and development arrangements
   - break and lunch periods, canteen facilities – and toilets
   - policies such as health and safety, company rules, leave of absence, training, education, promotion, disciplinary and grievance procedures (with copies, if available, to take away and digest)
   - guidelines as to expense claims, when and in what circumstances they may use company telephones and equipment such as computers, social and welfare arrangements, where they can obtain first aid.
3 Remember that new people will only be able to grasp a limited amount of information. Take your time explaining the above issues and ensure that you:
   - provide a folder with all available information
   - offer time, perhaps later in the week, to get together and talk over any issues or points that need clarification.
4 The new employee should then be taken to their place of work and introduced to someone responsible in that area for continuing the induction process – a line manager, for example. This person will also introduce them to their team/project group/peer group.

5   At this stage, the manager is likely to have chosen a member of his staff/team to continue the induction process. In my last company we operated a buddy system – the word 'buddy' seemed to capture just what a new person often needs in the early stages of employment. The buddy would:

- be someone who has a friendly manner, and perhaps be best described as a team worker
- be someone who would be a part of the new person's normal working environment
- be able to put the new person at ease
- be someone who was known to be generally supportive of the firm and/or the department/section/site
- provide basic information about specific working arrangements
- give information about the job
- be able to indicate and/or demonstrate standards of performance and appropriate work behaviour
- be able to tell the employee about training arrangements.

If the firm operates a mentor scheme, it may be appropriate to arrange a first meeting with a potential mentor during the first week (see the section titled 'The manager as mentor' later in this chapter).

Whoever is directly responsible for the employee should follow up – say, two weeks later – to check:

- whether the new person has settled into the company
- that their immediate working environment is conducive to gaining good performance
- that the job they thought they were being given is the one they are experiencing.

At this early stage of employment, the new person may not have sufficient confidence to be open about problems – especially if it involves people around them. Consequently, if you are not sure that you can provide an environment that is conducive to airing difficulties, it might be best to delegate the initial follow-up meeting to someone who is comparatively independent. For example, you might use a well-trained and professional personnel specialist who can have a confidential chat with the new employee. I always leave this initial follow-up meeting to someone else in the firm who I believe would act with integrity.

You can attract early employee interest and gain valuable public relations at the same time.

Finally, there is a view in the construction industry that larger firms might introduce themselves to primary and secondary schools, by giving school talks and facilitating site visits so that schoolchildren can explore the construction world as part of their education. Secondary school pupils might be given a taste for construction by involving them in more detailed experiences in the industry. It would seem that it's never too early to start the induction process if you are to attract the best people! Firms might also do well to engage with local further and higher education institutes to raise awareness of construction careers amongst both staff and students.

The manager as teambuilder and team leader

You may recall from the previous chapter that one of the most important motivators is the need to work and participate in social groups. Of course, as managers, we do not only want our people to work in groups; we want them to work together as a team in such a way that the overall performance of people is better. This effect is called synergy and is commonly described as 2+2=5. It means that the combined effect on performance exceeds the sum of individual performances. How can I explain this? Have you viewed those house-hunting programmes on TV? So often, the potential house owner is looking for that 'Wow factor'. That's what a high-performing team looks and feels like to you as their manager or team leader.

More specifically, teams can provide:

- support and help to members of the team
- ways of coordinating activities of team members
- commitment in the job leading to improved productivity and quality – members drive and enthuse each other
- on-the-job learning – members can encourage innovation, leading to extraordinary results
- a work setting that thrives on communication and is satisfying and enjoyable.

Building a team

There are a few implications of teamworking that demand certain management skills and knowledge. First, you need to know how to assemble a team and how to recruit suitable people into the team to ensure that it has a chance of performing like a team. So, the information contained in this section should form part of your recruitment and selection process.

Of course, you are going to need the right mix of skills – for example, bricklayers, plasterers, electricians, plumbers and so on. You also need to try to make sure that your people can work to an efficient standard. However, if you want a team to work well together and perhaps come up with new ideas, you also need to try to get the right behavioural competency mix. (Behavioural competencies were mentioned in Chapter 1.) You may need some expert help with this, but here are the fundamentals. People want to take on different roles in teams, at least partly because of their personality and partly because of what motivates or drives them. Put simply, too many people wanting to take on the same role means that other important roles might not be filled. Moreover, team members wanting the same role may challenge each other for it, and this can cause ongoing group conflict which prevents the team performing well. What can you do? Of course, you may know your people very well and be aware that a certain mix of personalities won't work. For example, some people may wish to control the team, or evaluate ideas, or provide the team with team spirit. Others will be intent on completing and finishing jobs – critical roles in the construction industry – whilst others tend to come up with ideas. The trick is to get a good match of people playing different roles and then bring them together to form a team.

There are questionnaires (similar to the personality profiling instruments mentioned earlier) that can help you identify which roles your people like to adopt. Various team role profiling instruments are available from many sources. The easiest way of finding them is to contact the CITB or simply search the Internet for 'personality questionnaires' adding the word 'teams'.

The interpretation of the questionnaires is all-important. So, consider going on a training course to learn how to use these instruments. If for no other reason, it would be good for your own personal/professional development. Alternatively, ask for specialist help. The result will be vital information about the make-up of your team, whether it lacks people with certain roles, has too many people wanting to adopt the same role, and/or whether you might develop certain people to take on certain team roles in the future to give the team greater balance.

Leading a team

How do you know that you are managing a team, rather than simply a group of individuals? It is best to look for signs of team development – or non-development, as the case may be. A group of people, rather than a true team, would show some of the following characteristics:

- poor discussion
- little questioning
- resistance to, or ignoring of, constructive ideas
- poor listening to you and/or other members
- blaming others when mistakes occur
- over-reliance on you, as manager, for making decisions.

You can improve or develop a team by trying out a few of the following:

1 Begin to involve people in the job.
2 Ask questions and listen to their answers.
3 If conflict exists between members, try to build a few bridges.
4 Develop problem-solving skills.
5 Celebrate team successes.

6   Give support.

7   Improve communication.

8   Allow conflicts to surface, but then seek common ground.

9   Get the team to regularly review performance.

10 Allow members to observe other people's jobs and ask how they may assist in making each job more effective.

Usually, if you handle the team development well, there will be:

- more communication (not just talk)
- better relationships within the team
- more trust between members and in you
- well-established and agreed rules and work practices
- a clear view of the team's purpose and objectives
- improved collecting and sharing of information
- constant and natural self-assessed review of performance
- more flexibility
- little defending of personal positions
- a clear demonstration of improved commitment to the team by members.

As a matter of interest, I have also found that, if I assemble and build my team on the above lines, they tend to work effectively without too much supervision, are happier to accept more responsibility, tend to work as a team in the sense that they are aware of other members' jobs and what they can do to help other members work, and conflict between members is an exception rather than the rule.

However, you need to be aware of a few barriers that can get in the way of team development:

It is not enough to improve the forces for improved teamwork – you have to reduce forces that can restrict improvement.

1   If you use poor recruitment and selection processes, you will be lucky to end up with suitable team members playing suitable team roles.

2   If you are unclear about the aims of the team, all you will get is a group of mystified individuals and guaranteed poor performance.

3   If you fail to control the team adequately, they can become too independent and become competitive with other teams.

4   Without appropriate training and development good teams cannot work well.

5   Although teams can help motivate members, if you as their manager or leader do not know how people are motivated, commitment to the job will be limited.

6   Unfair recognition, rewards and incentives can stifle team performance.

If you are the team leader, you should follow the guidelines below:

1   Be consistent and act with integrity at all times.

2 Try to select members of the team who will fit the team – use team role profiling as mentioned above.

3 Develop your team members (there is more about development in Chapter 4).

4 Build a positive work environment. It's all about leadership style, recognition and so on, as discussed in Chapter 2.

5 Give attention to motivation by achievement. When the team achieves, give credit and praise when and where it is due. Make sure that your own boss knows how well the team has done and make sure that they congratulate your team.

6 If performance is poor, try to review it with the team without casting blame. Work positively on how you might improve the situation; then acknowledge and celebrate improvement.

The importance of teambuilding and development is well accepted in the construction industry. However, it is also recognized that, to successfully complete many projects, people from different teams – and, indeed, different firms – need to join together. In construction there is now a growing need for integrated teams and supply chains. The benefits of working towards efficient and effective integrated teams are advocated via the *Rethinking Construction* and *Accelerating Change* initiatives. A cross-company best-case example would be staff seconded from BAA, AMEC and other second-tier suppliers. They share office facilities where IT and administrative support is provided. The aim is to enable 'best value' for money. Performance outcomes are impressive. Capital costs are down by 30 per cent over five years, and construction time is shorter, with consistent delivery on time – 'to programme'. In addition, productivity is well above the industry average, but not at the expense of the accident rate which is amongst the lowest in the UK. This team is fully integrated and meets the need of a virtual company. Of course, all that has previously been said about the need to mix and match team members' skills, knowledge and personal characteristics appropriately and to develop teams holds true for virtual companies as well as more conventional single-company and single-function teams.

Team briefings

Team briefings should not be boring or one-sided.

Your company may operate a team briefing process whereby you formally meet your team on a regular basis (usually once a month) and present, receive and discuss information about the firm. The information provided is usually prepared by senior management to be delivered throughout the company to all people. Team briefings are normally chaired, and the information is delivered by the team leader. The subjects covered – and hopefully discussed – include:

- company performance, including financial results – for example, month-end sales figures, cost information, new and important sales contracts (such as building contracts) and so on

- plans – for instance, the why, how and immediate and longer-term implications of internal re-structuring
- people – new appointments and issues related to pay and conditions
- new or revised policies – for example, equality and diversity policy.

You may have noticed my use of the words 'hopefully discussed'. I have experienced so many team briefings that appear to exclude, or do not even invite, discussion. In such circumstances, I have been observing a meeting of a group of individuals rather than a team. It is supposed to be a two-way communication process! I have even known occasions when the manager was simply reading from a script without knowing what the words actually meant. Perhaps an example will help. It is normal in team briefings for company results to be conveyed – for example, 'profits the company made in the last quarter'. It is not uncommon to see that all present listen intensively. Some may nod in approval; others may wait to see whether the majority nod before deciding how they might respond. Is the profit figure given 'gross' or 'before tax'? It makes a big difference. On one occasion I asked the team leader what profit level the brief was referring to. There was a very distinct and uncomfortable silence, leaving me in little doubt that I shouldn't have asked the question. Yet, what is the use of information if your people do not understand it? Furthermore, what is the likelihood that information will be received or acted on if no one understands it? Worse still, what if people convey or act on the information in a totally inappropriate way? It is worth remembering that if the company has a team structure, team members attending the briefing may also lead their own teams and cascade (possibly wrong) information to members of their own teams. If there is no opportunity to comment on issues raised by the briefing, there is a greater chance of the information causing confusion. A simple rule is that the briefing should be worded or explained so that it can be understood and commented on by everyone, should they wish to do so.

Team briefings can be a very effective way of eliciting important comments and ideas from members of teams – allowing for communication up, down and across the organization. Clearly, they work best when real teams have been designed, developed and are well led.

The manager's toolbox of skills

There is little doubt that the best firms in the construction industry are those that have identified and have helped develop critical management skills. Appropriate use of management skills make a substantial contribution to company performance. I have already mentioned skills such as time management, interviewing, meetings management and so on. Construction industry companies also rely

The manager's toolbox of advanced skills: trainer, coach, mentor and counsellor.

heavily on the ability of managers to apply man or person management skills. For example, if you want the respect of your staff, there is nothing better than being willing to involve yourself in their jobs and their careers, to take part in their training, or to make that crucial but personal intervention just when they need it. Unfortunately, training, being a mentor, coaching or having the confidence and knowledge about how and when to counsel people is not simple. Even the skill of presenting does not come naturally to many managers in the construction industry. Like so many valued manager skills, 'presenting' can be very stressful, so you have to learn how and when to do it.

When working to improve people performance little that is worthwhile comes easy, but the rewards in terms of job satisfaction can be considerable. If you have worked through previous sections of this book – for example, sections on communicating, recruiting and gaining commitment – and wondered what manager skills are involved, look no further; here they are.

The manager as trainer

Training people requires the right approach and structure, appropriate knowledge, applicable communication skills and – above all, confidence. The latter is the most difficult to achieve. It might be worth mentioning that the most effective trainers I have seen look superbly confident but, in actual fact, would admit that they are never completely confident – anxiety remains, but is controlled. It is my guess that a little well-directed anxiety is something that excellent trainers/presenters make good use of. Their anxiety tends to concentrate their minds on the prime objective of the activity, that is how can they ensure that people learn from the experience?

Delivering learning effectively

There are, in fact, key factors about people that enable them to learn effectively:

Learn how best to help your people learn.

- People learn best when they see a worthwhile end-product. They need an incentive, or at least a good reason, for the training.
- Learning must be relevant. How many times have you attended a training event and wished you were somewhere else?
- Doing promotes understanding. Don't just talk at people; when possible, give them something to do, even if you only ask them to think about what has been said and tell you how it might be achieved in the workplace.
- People need freedom to make mistakes. OK, I know what you're thinking – whatever happened to that 'get it right first time' stuff? Well, if what is being learnt is really crucial, make sure that you can simulate it within a training environment.

Clearly, some mistakes can be costly – in terms of money, time or health. You need to use your judgement. Otherwise, making mistakes can be an excellent way of learning. Can you remember how you learnt not to stall a car at the traffic lights? Did you make mistakes? If you did, how did reflection about stalling help you get it right?

- People need feedback (discussed earlier in this chapter). Some managers have never heard of the word 'feedback'. It simply means to review worker performance and tell them how they did. Within a training session giving and receiving feedback can be a valuable tool.
- New knowledge and/or skills is best absorbed at the learner's own pace. People learn at different rates and in different ways.

This last point brings me back to an important issue: before you set about training or presenting you need to know your audience. To this end, ask yourself some key questions:

1   Who are my audience?
2   What are their expectations?
3   What incentive can I give?
4   What kind of language should I use?
5   How much information can they take in at any time? (Remember, if you know something well you tend to overestimate other people's ability to absorb the knowledge you are trying to convey.)

Accept that:

- People must be motivated to learn.
- They must know the standards of performance you expect them to achieve.
- Learners need guidance or, better still, a demonstration of what you mean.
- For learning to take place and for the newly acquired knowledge or skill to be useful in the workplace, learners need to feel satisfied with the event or process – otherwise they will retain knowledge of the learning experience but will be reluctant to apply it to their job.

You can meet these learning needs by following these guidelines:

- Use appropriate techniques. If the learning is skill-based, don't just lecture them.
- Use a variety of learning methods. Remember that most people learn in different ways, so use discussion, videos, a case study, group work, on- and off-the-job reinforcement and so on.
- Allow time for reflection and comment.
- Review the process and the content.

How to present yourself effectively

In presenting yourself effectively you face two challenges:

1   the presence of other people
2   getting yourself and your message across.

You have only four things to think about:

1   how you look
2   how you move
3   how you speak
4   what you say.

As for your physical and visual impact, consider the following:

- Appearance: neat, tidy, clean, suitably dressed.
- Stance and bearing: erect but relaxed.
- Positioning: for focus and impact.
- Movement and gestures: bold, purposeful – avoiding mannerisms if possible.
- Facial expression: mobile, smiling, not too serious, not too frivolous.

As for vocal impact, consider the following:

- Voice: make it audible, strong, pleasant, varied.
- Diction: shape words clearly, open mouth – don't mumble.
- Emphasis: hit words hard – especially those you see as key words.
- Tune: let your voice rise and fall naturally – avoid monotone delivery.
- Pace: slow at the start, then vary for impact.
- Pause: use to 'punctuate' sense.
- Tone: reflect feeling.

Prepare what you need to say, but listen and try to think before you speak. Most importantly, choose words suitable to your audience. Confidence is, of course, 'half the battle', but repetition, practice and, above all, preparation can help. Let me give you an example. My daughter came to me last night, saying that she had to do a 20-minute presentation and asking how she should go about it, because she felt so nervous. I suggested that she provide herself with a plan, write the plan down on A4 paper using big writing and then practise in front of a sympathetic and constructive audience – which turned out to be me. Quite simply, you need to build your confidence by providing yourself with a plan and preparing for your talk or presentation. In this way, you give yourself a structure to work through – something like this:

1 **Introduction**: introduce yourself, what you are going to talk about and why, your or the organization's aims, an incentive to listen.
2 **Main body**: explain points, focus on key issues, check for understanding as you work through each point, summarize clusters of points.
3 **Main summary**: use to reinforce key headings/clusters of key points.
4 **Consolidation**: perhaps invite questions and clarify issues.
5 **Conclusion**: refer to the future – what you expect will happen now – thank the audience and maybe offer some final remarks.

Teaching practical skills

Of course, managers in the construction industry will often be involved in teaching practical or manual skills. Here are a few basic guidelines:

'To teach: to enable a person to do something by instruction' (Oxford English Dictionary)

1 **Prepare**:
– Do the job or rehearse the subject before instruction begins.
– Divide the task/activity into stages.
– Select key points, for example, safety factors.
– Get everything ready – room layout, materials, equipment, visual aids and so on.

2 **Instruct**:
– Put people at their ease.
– Explain what the job/activity/task is.
– Check for existing knowledge/experience.
– Create interest in learning how to do the activity/task.
– Tell, show and illustrate the task/activity – one step at a time.
– Make clear the important points – for example, safety issues.
– Instruct clearly and patiently.
– Give essential information at a suitable pace – not all at once.

3 **Try out**:
– Get the trainee to explain the subject and/or try out the task/activity.
– Correct errors as they occur.
– Check that the trainee understands the important points.
– Continue until you are satisfied with the trainee's performance.

4 **Conclude**:
– State what personal responsibilities the trainee has.
– Provide the trainee with the name of a trusted person in the workplace who they can speak with.
– Encourage questions.
– Review performance (on the job).

The manager as coach

Coaching is a means of helping your people focus on what is really important in their job.

The numbers of craft, technical, administrative, supervisory and management skills required in the construction industry and the need to continuously update these skills makes the act of coaching crucial to the overall performance of the firm. Coaching is a process that develops staff at the same time as getting the job done. It is concerned with improved job performance and is central to improving the effectiveness of the business. It does so by systematically increasing competence through giving planned tasks, with counselling and control provided by the manager. It is a means of:

- developing staff while at the same time getting the job done
- increasing the ability and experience of the employee by giving planned tasks, with counselling and control provided by the manager
- using the job itself to improve skills, knowledge and performance
- empowering people by devolving responsibility
- improving and/or extending people's motivation and improving morale and hence productivity and overall company performance.

Through the coaching process the manager enables learning opportunities and helps with reflection on planned experiences. The manager skills required include searching questions, discussion, encouragement, providing information, and giving and receiving feedback. The coaching process also requires interpersonal skill development, dedicated time and a willingness to incorporate the process on a regular basis.

Coaching skills include:

1 *Observation*: standing back dispassionately to review the situation.
2 *Active listening*: not just hearing but making an effort to understand; being able to empathize.
3 *Discussion*: the coach may need to challenge and confront.
4 *Questioning*: to seek clarification and to encourage two-way discussion.
5 *Summarizing*: used to check for agreement.
6 *Problem-solving*: coaching can be most effective when focused on an agreed work problem or the need for a specific improvement in performance.
7 *Suggesting*: offering options' ideas or a different approach.
8 *Delegation*: transferring responsibility to the employee – easier said than done!

Some managers tend to be apathetic towards coaching, arguing the importance of other more pressing priorities and a lack of immediate results. However, such views are probably atypical of good managers. Coaching must be viewed as important, and be driven, by senior management at the top of the organization. If you want to encourage the coaching process in your firm, it is best to concentrate on its clear and important benefits to the firm:

- better teamwork
- improved performance
- broader outlook of coachee
- more job satisfaction for both coachee and coach
- personal development of both parties.

However, effective coaching requires:

- coaching champions
- sufficient time
- clear objectives
- an appropriate method
- full agreement of both parties
- an appropriate organizational climate
- clear standards of effectiveness
- access to appropriate training programmes
- evaluation and feedback – again, time can be an issue.

In my experience, coaching is a manager's best means of improving individual, and even team, performance. Unfortunately, it relies on five key factors:

1 Has the manager got the time to coach?
2 Does the organization recognize the benefit of coaching?
3 Has the manager been trained in coaching techniques?
4 Has the manager the necessary people skills to make coaching effective?
5 Will employees react favourably to the idea?

You may find that your management style fits nicely with the coaching process. For instance, it may feel natural for you to provide your people with new ideas or better ways of carrying out their responsibilities/tasks, and give regular feedback about their performance. Being a good coach usually means being friendly, accessible, considerate and naturally interested in developing people. I have found that the best coaches are natural developers of other people; they look out for ways to improve performance through people, they watch how people do their job and have an inherent interest in providing guidance.

You may recall my comments on management/leadership style in Chapter 2. Coaches are normally more 'people-' rather than 'task-centred'. That is not to say that coaches think that 'getting the job done' is unimportant; it is simply that they see the development of people's competency as the best means of improving work performance. You may feel that these skills, management style and developmental attitude are qualities you need to acquire. Fortunately, there are several off-the-job training courses available that can provide you with an opportunity to practise questioning, observational and interpersonal communication skills. Normally, these courses allow you to play the role of coach as well as being coached by a professional practitioner. This helps you experience both roles and reflect and comment on the experience in a safe 'training' environment. I recommend attendance.

The manager as mentor

Generally speaking, the use of mentoring may be limited to medium and large organizations in the construction industry. It is particularly useful for construction companies that rely on timely succession planning – where it is important that middle and senior managers 'hit their new job running'.

While coaching can build performance in the short term, mentoring is concerned with the longer-term perspective. It refers to the building of a relationship between an experienced manager who can share their experience, guide behaviour, and provide feedback to a protégé. The focus of the process is the need to improve people's performance.

Younger people need an experienced and positive role model.

A mentor is best described as an experienced and trusted adviser who is normally not the trainee's line manager and may be a manager in a different department or different part of the firm. The protégé (sometimes referred to as the mentored or mentoree) is someone who is normally new to the company and who hopes to benefit from being mentored by the experienced manager.

As a training and development tool, mentoring is not new. For centuries wise men and women have offered counsel to the young. It is generally accepted that mentoring done well can offer a wide range of advantages to both protégé and mentor.

The mentor role may be summarized as follows:

1 The mentor provides the trainee (protégé) with the opportunity, through discussion, to look objectively at their performance and ongoing development. The mentor should encourage the trainee to examine their perceptions of the company, department/place of work, and themselves.
2 The mentor must be able to share with the trainee a broad awareness of the business and its objectives.
3 The mentor does not take away the responsibility of a trainee's line manager, who remains responsible for ensuring that the trainee is effectively utilized, trained and developed.
4 While the confidentiality of the mentor–trainee relationship should be maintained, there may be occasions when the mentor believes that some form of corrective action is required, as a

result of, for example, disenchantment with a training programme, underutilization of skills or knowledge and so on.

Mentoring involves:

1 *Sponsorship*: this usually constitutes a decision by senior management that the mentoring process can have medium- to long-term benefits, especially in terms of succession planning and career progression.
2 *Coaching*: a mentor requires the same skills as highlighted above.
3 *Challenging dialogue and challenging work*: perhaps developmental project work.

Mentors should be:

Mentor: Wise, Trusted, Adviser, Guide.

- shrewd listeners
- able to relate/interpret what the protégé says to some other wider awareness
- individuals who have developed a well defined philosophy of life
- able to ask many varied, but appropriate, questions
- a counsellor (more about this role below)
- a networker – someone who has extensive internal links with other influential people in the organization and good relations with others outside the organization
- a facilitator who knows how and when to get things done – they are politically astute (understanding and able to work with internal company politics, procedures, policies and so on).

Mentors are often seen within the firm as good role models for new recruits to the business – for example, a person you might point out to a new employee as someone they may wish to emulate. Mentors are normally able to strike up a friendship with most people; they have integrity, are sincere and loyal (committed to the company); they are also honest and can 'open doors' that would otherwise have remained closed to the protégé.

I have only known a few exceptional mentors and only had the privilege of being mentored by one. However, that relationship lasted for nearly five years. How does the concept work? Well, quite simply, the mentor and protégé get together to discover whether they can get along. If the first meetings are favourable, there will be open discussions about the company, its internal and external context (issues covered in Chapter 1, perhaps), discussions about the protégé's aspirations, and agreement as to the objectives of the process from the points of view of both parties. From there on, the dialogue and regularity of the discussions is in the hands of the two parties as are the projects, activities, experiential learning events and so on that the parties view as supportive of the protégé's development and career progression. The benefits can be listed as follows:

- increased job satisfaction experienced by both mentor and protégé
- career advice and development
- increased self-confidence
- a broader awareness of the business, including aspects that are normally not discussed – for example, company politics.

Unlike coaching, practical training on becoming a mentor is difficult to find – probably because the skills and behaviour of effective mentors take a lifetime to develop. It is therefore easier to look around for natural mentors within the company.

Meetings between mentors and protégés should conform to the following guidelines:

1 *Frequency*. I suggest that the mentor and protégé should meet on a bi-monthly basis.
2 *Arrangement of meetings*. The onus is on the protégé to arrange the first meeting. Thereafter, further meetings can be arranged at the end of each meeting.
3 *Topics for discussion*. These should include job-related issues; broader issues, such as the future of the company and new initiatives; personal issues – for example, training, development, career aspirations, motivation, commitment and so on.
4 *Length of the relationship/partnership*. If the protégé is also a new graduate, then the arrangement should continue at least until the end of their probation or development period – perhaps one year.
5 *Controls/review*. Each meeting should be informally recorded by the protégé and used to help structure the agenda of each meeting. Notes can assist the protégé when involved in the appraisal process – setting objectives, development and so on. Although the mentoring process is usually confidential between the mentor and protégé, the content via the protégé, and with their permission, can be used to inform appraisals, performance reviews, learning contracts, training and development plans and so on.

The manager as counsellor

To recap, mentoring is concerned with providing the protégé with a sponsor to assist their career, while coaching is directly related to improving people's performance. Counselling, however, normally focuses on personal issues and/or problems. All three skills affect performance. In many ways, although counselling is arguably the most difficult skill for a manager to develop and use effectively, it can have the most beneficial effect on people's performance. Let me say from the outset that, if you are interested in developing counselling techniques, there are several reputable courses readily available.

Counselling can assist people in resolving their problems – but you need training before you attempt it.

Perhaps counselling and the construction industry do not make obvious bedfellows. Counselling is the softest management skill, and construction often sees itself as a very macho industry. Nevertheless, counselling and respect for people do make good bedfellows. As mentioned by the *Rethinking Construction* partners, respect for people is ultimately a two-way thing. Showing respect to our workforce, while simultaneously winning respect from them yields results that benefit everyone.

Counselling is a technique (or a number of related manager competencies) through which one person helps another person examine and solve their own problems. Here, I must issue a warning. I am making no suggestion that managers should see themselves as professional counsellors – for example, to try to be clinical stress counsellors and start advising about matters outside the workplace and outside their remit. If a manager spots that an employee has real difficulties with, say, alcohol abuse, distress or violent behaviour, they should call on professional help. Many organizations employ specialist and highly qualified counsellors. However, a manager's responsibility is to notice any deterioration in work performance and respond to alleviate the cause, and many situations occur within the workplace that managers might see and intervene using a counselling approach.

Counselling involves:

- listening, using silence, sharing, probing, clarifying, reflecting, summarizing and, when appropriate, referring
- ethics and the adoption of a non-directive and anti-discriminatory approach
- integrity, respect and impartiality
- privacy and confidentiality.

> *'Well-timed silence hath more eloquence than speech.' (Martin Fraquhar Tupper)*

In a typical counselling event/process you would need to do the following:

- Establish rapport.
- Allow the ventilation of feelings.
- Get agreement that a problem exists.
- Get the individual to explore options/solutions.
- Agree on action to be taken – not necessarily only by the individual as issues might relate to others or processes related to the company.
- Hold follow-up meetings to check for improvements in the individual's situation. The chances are the counsellor/manager will be able to gather objective evidence, such as improvements in attendance, timekeeping, observable behaviour and so on.
- Recognize the individual's achievement when it occurs. Simply apply some positive strokes to encourage the improvement.

Establishing rapport is arguably more important within a potential counselling situation. If a climate of trust and confidentiality cannot be established it is unlikely that the root cause of poor performance will be ascertained. The following ideas may be useful:

- Maintain a warm and friendly manner.
- Treat the other person as an equal.
- Ensure that the counselling environment is right – no interruptions, guaranteed privacy, non-judgemental or confrontational. Avoid talks 'across the boss's desk'.
- Maintain a non-judgemental and non-confrontational manner.
- Allow as much time as it will take. And, again from experience, double it.
- Do not assume an interview or disciplinary approach.
- Show a sympathetic interest.
- Give your full attention – don't start looking at your watch!
- Again, as with so many managerial skills, listen actively not passively. Always follow what the speaker is saying attentively, giving verbal or non-verbal signals to indicate that you are listening – for example 'Mmm', 'I see', 'Go on' or nodding or shaking the head. Take care to keep in mind the thread of what they are saying and to give them time to reflect on what they have said. Then, when appropriate, try to identify the main themes, message and/or concerns and summarize these back to the speaker for confirmation – for example, 'So you feel angry with your supervisor because …'.
- Be sensitive to, and conscious of, those tell-tale non-verbal clues that often lead to uncovering the root cause of the problem – as they see it. Try to keep in mind that, to them, the problem is serious enough for it to alter their behaviour and affect their work performance. You are dealing with their perception of a problem – not yours.

The above list is probably sufficient for any reader to accept the fact that they need to adopt a very professional approach. Let me reiterate, if you are in doubt as to whether you possess the right skills and attitude, do not attempt to counsel – get someone who is trained and who you respect to do it. That is not to say that you should abdicate responsibility; your responsibility remains regardless of whether or not you ask a specialist to conduct the counselling role. This is particularly important if you accept that there are times when you, as the individual's manager, are the only one who can do something to eradicate the barriers that might be preventing the individual from performing effectively. Also, if you decide not to counsel, you should welcome advice and comment from the person chosen to be the counsellor, before, and most definitely after, the counselling session.

Final thoughts about using the manager's toolbox of skills

You may have noticed that certain skills are used (to a lesser or greater extent) when giving training presentations, providing coaching, acting as a mentor and counselling – for example, feedback skills, questioning skills and listening skills. Rather than immersing yourself in a fully blown counselling course (which could take one year), you may wish to attend short training courses and test out your newly found skills in a gradual way. My advice is that, if in doubt, speak with your manager, get some training and seek advice, if available, from personnel/human resource specialists. Even if you feel confident about conducting coaching and counselling sessions, without destroying confidentiality, always tell a personnel officer/manager that you are doing it – you may need their help later.

Although this may be stating the obvious, make sure that you are aware of company policies and personnel procedures on such aspects as employment policies, equal opportunity, managing diversity, pay, employee relations, health and safety, sexual harassment, discrimination, smoking policy, drug abuse and so on. These documents provide essential management support and guidance.

Retaining people

Monitoring staff turnover is important to business success. High turnover leads to difficulty maintaining customer–client relationships. In a project setting you should also consider the unplanned turnover of your subcontracted teams. The impact of high turnover on project performance is similar to that on the company – delays in production, quality problems, customer service problems, client dissatisfaction, profit issues and so on. Clearly, small companies and small subcontractors in the construction industry feel the impact of high turnover more than larger concerns. The industry median in 2001 was around 9 per cent. Benchmarked 2003 figures indicate around 7 per cent average turnover (all sizes of organization).

Currently there is high employment in the UK; in such a situation more of your people may leave to join other companies. This may especially be so if they perceive that they will have better opportunities for advancement elsewhere. Moreover, regardless of the employment situation, some of your staff will leave or retire, so you can be certain that there will be a degree of staff turnover. Most organizations appreciate a small turnover of staff, but not too many because it can cause damaging operational problems. I realize that you might be quite content to lose or 'reluctantly let go' some of your people, as you can use the opportunity of a small turnover of people to recruit and select the best available people from the marketplace. Replacing certain people with others who may be more committed to their work, their team and/or the company is always a possibility.

It is also true that, despite your best efforts, some of your best people will leave the company. However, your job is to try to retain them. This section provides a few ideas. You will not be surprised to find that in order to retain your best people, you must adopt several of the good ideas and management practices already discussed. Here are a few that I have tried and have found, on reflection, to have provided fair results.

1   *Recruitment and selection.* If you recruit and select the wrong people at the wrong time to do the wrong job, don't be surprised when they say they want to leave. I am always amazed that managers put so little effort into recruitment and selection. Some say that the exercise uses too much of their time and it's costly. My response is to ask them how much it costs to recruit the wrong people. Apart from recruitment and salary costs, can you imagine how much it costs to recruit one person who never performs well, makes mistakes, sours the working environment for others and then stays with the company because they have few other alternatives? I suggest you refer to the advice given earlier in the chapter about how to help recruit and select the best people.

2   *Rewards and incentives.* Although we might agree that pay is a hygiene factor and not a motivation factor (see Chapter 2), nevertheless it is important. There are a few things you can do:

 - Review pay levels by assessing current market rates – what are your competitors paying their best people?
 - Involve your people in job evaluation or re-evaluation processes/schemes to make sure that they are paid for the job they do on an equitable basis.
 - Review your performance-related pay scheme (if your company has one) and make sure that it is both fair and operated well, and that your best employees are being rewarded.
 - Ask your best people whether they feel they are getting an adequate level of pay for the job that they do. You might expect that everyone wants more money, and that, of course, is true. Nevertheless, I have found that if you phrase the question using the words 'for the job you do', you often get a more accurate response. What you are trying to do is find out what your people perceive as a fair wage.
 - Consider whether you can adapt payment-by-results schemes to ensure that your best people benefit.
 - If you recall the essence of Chapter 2, all motivations can be used as an incentive. Use them extensively.

3 Training *and development*. Expect your best people to leave if they are continuously asked to perform well when they have not been trained and/or developed. Make sure that your people hold appropriate levels of knowledge, skill and behavioural competence to do what they are being requested to do. Moreover, don't forget that your best people will expect to be developed. Support for educational development can aid staff retention. In my experience, good performance comes from people who have a need to achieve and do their jobs well. However, they need confidence to take on new demands, projects, responsibilities and the like, and that is precisely what training, development and education can help provide. More about the importance of training and development in Chapter 4.

4 *Career development and succession planning*. If your best workers are achievers, they will probably want to develop their career. If their career stagnates, they will leave to find better opportunities elsewhere – perhaps to your competitors. Obviously, your best people have the best chance of leaving – such is life. Lifelong employment 'from cradle to grave' with one organization appears to be a concept of the past. Nevertheless, if you have spent time and money developing good people, it makes sense to get the most out of them while they are still employed by your company – anyway, that's your job. Here are a few things I do – sometimes as part of annual appraisals, sometimes via informal chats or coaching sessions:

'Good people do not need laws to tell them to act responsively, while bad people will find a way around the laws.'
(Plato)

- Provide advice about career opportunities. This is more difficult than it sounds, because your advice may entail them leaving your part of the company for another part. Selfishly, you may wish to make opportunities and career paths that are open (or may become open) in your 'neck of the woods' known first. Nevertheless, you should encourage promotion of your best people within your own company.
- Work with the central HR department (if you have one) to ensure that your best people are known to the organization as a whole, and that they are seen and noted as 'people of potential'.
- Consider using some of the abilities mentioned earlier under the role of mentor.
- Sit down with your best people and discuss their aspirations and work needs. This is the most obvious idea, but one that so many managers neglect.
- One word of warning – never promise new job opportunities if you think you cannot deliver them. Never raise expectations so far that the only way is to let people down. Raise people's interest but be honest with them.

5   *Good management.* As management development manager of a major multinational, I held quite a few 'exit interviews' with people who had previously been earmarked as future senior managers or senior engineers. It was an interesting experience just to counsel people leaving the company and try to find out why they were leaving. Of course, some were going because their spouse had received an unrefusable job opportunity in some other part of the country or world, some left to have children and wanted to spend their first few years with them, others wanted to emigrate to a warmer climate – not a bad idea! Out of all that were leaving because of work reasons, you may be surprised to know that 'more pay' was actually quite low down compared to poor management. It seemed that most people started looking for a new job elsewhere because they 'did not rate their manager' – it was only then that some even became aware of opportunities for more pay outside their firm. Some tips:

  – Give people recognition. Have another look at the section on recognition in Chapter 2 – it constitutes far more than giving praise.
  – Talk with your people on a regular basis – walk the job.
  – Take the opportunity to discuss work needs and aspirations during performance agreement, appraisals and coaching sessions, and give balanced feedback.
  – Discuss performance problems (should they occur) as early as possible (see Chapter 4). One of the best indicators that your best people are losing interest is when they suddenly start to make mistakes, come in late and frequently miss a day's work – watch their behaviour.
  – Make sure there are no outstanding issues related to 1, 2, 3 and 4 above.

If I could only pick one of the above five management practices, I would always pick 'good management'. Perhaps, like me, you have experience of being managed well. Although I can't remember always wanting to go to work, I do remember when I did not mind so much. At such times, you feel involved, have some authority, know your job responsibilities, and you can talk to the boss. You also feel you are getting and receiving appropriate development and a fair salary for the job. Your abilities are used appropriately. This is not to say that you always get your own way all the time, but the boss listens, supports you and appreciates your efforts. In general, you derive a great deal of satisfaction from the job.

What did the best manager you have ever known do to make you think he or she was the best?

You may wish to think about the best manager you have known and make a list of the characteristics, competencies and people management abilities that that person displayed. It is also a good idea to make a list of the characteristics of the worst manager you have known and then compare both lists. I guess the list of the 'best manager you have known' (or currently know) contains both good management and effective leadership qualities. Was I right?

Summary

In this chapter we have looked at how to create a working environment that encourages and maintains high performance. We have seen that this process starts by making sure that the company mission states where the organization is going. Moreover, the objectives and values contained in the statement must be understood by, and acceptable to, all employees, as well as to all other stakeholders of the firm. We also considered the need for appropriate communication. A discussion of various methods and techniques concentrated on the need for effective communication and, in particular, your role as a communicator and receiver of information.

We then looked at creating the right mix of attitudes and skills for high performance and your role, as manager, in recruiting and selecting the right people and then in building and leading effective teams. But having the right people with the appropriate skills in place is not enough. People need to feel job satisfaction to perform well – they need to be happy in their work. Your personal skills, as a manager, are critical to this. Competency in the so-called 'soft' management skills of coaching, mentoring and counselling all go a long way towards keeping team members on course and productive.

But what does high performance look like? How do you know when you've got it? And, more importantly, how do you keep it going? The next chapter looks in more detail at the methods of performance management.

Chapter **4**

Performance Management Methods

Introduction

To remain competitive in today's world, a company needs to continually review and improve its performance. Its people need to be motivated and willing to deliver that improved performance. Your ability to help your people gain job satisfaction from achieving the company's goals depends on whether they feel that they matter and that their contribution is recognized. Chapter 3 considered strategies that can greatly assist job satisfaction – for example, the importance of people seeing how their work fits within the firm's strategic plans, the importance of appropriate and timely communication, the need for people to receive feedback, your role in making sure that they work in a team and so on. Personal skills can also be used for decisive advantage; hence the section describing the manager's toolbox of skills. So, the next challenge for you, as manager, is how do you keep up the momentum?

The questions you need to ask yourself are:

- Do we use our performance process effectively?
- Are my people being developed to their full potential in their existing jobs?

In this chapter we look at performance management methods, starting with performance agreements and objective-setting and how performance is measured and monitored, including benchmarking. The kind of performance measures used can sometimes reveal all sorts of hidden problems. Of course, it is your job, as manager, to evaluate individual performance, so sections on individual behavioural performance and appraisal techniques are included.

Continuous improvement is impossible if skills are not kept up-to-date and relevant, so we go on to review the training and development process from identifying training needs and job evaluation through training plans to training provision. Development is, of course, a way of helping satisfy an individual's need for recognition as well as a means of ensuring that they work to their full potential. Clearly, it's your responsibility to develop both yourself and your people.

Nevertheless, in the best-run companies problems and conflicts will arise from time to time. The trick is to spot them in time, know how to identify their causes and, of course, put them right! Consequently, the final section of this chapter shows you how to deal with any performance problems that might be getting in the way of your goal of improving people performance.

Performance agreements and setting objectives

First, let me make a few comments about performance objectives, goals and measures. Performance objectives are something that the firm must achieve. If it does not achieve them, the company would significantly decrease customer satisfaction, system performance, employee satisfaction or retention, financial strength and so on. A performance goal is a target that is expressed in number form or in qualitative terms that can be measured – for example, actual net profit compared with forecasted net profit, actual sales compared with forecasted sales, actual costs as compared with budgeted costs, levels of customer satisfaction against a predetermined desired level. Performance management is the process you use to effect positive changes based on the results of performance measurement.

Chapter 2 mentioned the motivational effect of knowing and agreeing goals and objectives. Without them, teams and individuals will find it difficult to achieve and receive recognition for their achievement. Clearly, performance agreements and the setting of performance objectives is part of the performance management process, so, first, let me briefly state a few important principles of effective performance management:

1 You, as manager, accept ownership of the performance management process, but all involved act as partners to make sure that it is successful.
2 Performance management should apply to all people, not just a select few.
3 Although the structure of performance management is generic (it fits all firms, markets, industries) you need to ensure that it is adapted and is flexible enough to meet your specific company objectives. Give particular attention to specific performance measures, sometimes called key performance indicators (KPIs). They represent both standards of performance and a means of measuring performance.
4 You should concentrate on people or team improvement plans, but make sure that they are in line with company objectives.
5 Plans must be reviewed and, if your people's performance is related to pay, then ensure that the process provides suitable data in order to rate each person or team.

Your responsibilities therefore include:

- *Setting and agreeing performance.* A performance contract or agreement is a written formal document that records agreement. It simply states what individuals and teams reporting to you need to achieve. It will take the form of a list of agreed performance measures or indicators and will state agreed targets (explained later). It must also say how performance will be measured (usually by referring to known measures and agreed objectives) and what competencies will be required of the individual or team to achieve desired results.

- *Setting a development plan.* This written document sets out personal development needs. Usually, personal needs are written into an agreed personal development plan or perhaps a learning contract.

- *Monitoring performance and giving feedback.* Using the performance contract and development plan, you need to monitor performance and give each individual and team feedback. This should occur during the term of the contract and development plan – normally once a month over a one-year period. Usually, this is an informal process that you can simply make a part of your everyday manager activity of reviewing progress and, if appropriate, dealing with shortfalls in performance.

- *Reviewing performance.* You will also be responsible for conducting a more formal review of performance – usually once per quarter or once per year. If you are involved in projects, you may be able to design formal review meetings as part of the project schedule. Again, using the performance contract and personal or team development plans, you should review performance and consider any need to revise them. You might also use this review for rating the performance of individuals and/or team for the purpose of calculating performance-related pay (discussed in Chapter 2).

As your company may be new to some of the above ideas, following further explanation, usable template forms are provided later in this chapter.

Performance agreements must clearly state agreed objectives and how performance will be measured. They may also include the competencies needed to successfully achieve objectives. Agreements may be linked with individual and team development plans (covered later in this chapter). All this may sound like a lot of work. However, when critical objectives are set appropriately they help you in one very important way – your people know what is expected of them. If you do not set them, you are likely to find yourself involved in an argument about what performance level/target was actually agreed. You may win the argument by virtue of being the boss, but you risk destroying your people's commitment. When it comes to reviewing performance, agreements provide evidence that can be used as a foundation for reasoned dialogue.

If you can't measure it, you can't improve it.

Just a word about what an objective looks like. It is something (usually a target) that must be delivered or accomplished. It must clearly say what your part of the organization, your team or your people need to achieve. When designing objectives, I use a well-known method called SMART. The letters ask you to make sure that when setting objectives they are:

S – **S**tretching

M – **M**easurable

A – **A**greed

R – **R**ealistic and Relevant

T – **T**ime-bounded (indicating when the objective must be completed)

An example of a SMART objective might be: 'The team will reduce costs per unit by 3 per cent by the end of the current financial year – ending 30 April 20XX.' Here, of course, I am assuming that you would agree that the objective is stretching, but realistic, and that you have agreed it with your team. If so, then this is a good objective to work towards. A team that achieved a 1 per cent reduction in costs in the current financial year or a 3 per cent reduction at the end of the next financial year will have underperformed.

Clearly, objectives that are quantifiable are easier to set and monitor than objectives that are known as qualitative – for example, that a customer complaint is dealt with efficiently and in a friendly manner to the customer's satisfaction. Such an objective is probably stretching but not easy to measure. It may have been agreed and, if the firm is to stay in business, it is obviously relevant and realistic to expect your team to achieve it; however, it is an ongoing objective – it is something the team or individuals must achieve today, tomorrow, next week or next month. The timeframe is one that carries on as long as the company continues to trade.

Performance measures/indicators (KPIs)

Sir John Egan's report, *Rethinking Construction* (1998) concluded that, if the construction industry is to meet new challenges and opportunities, it must transform itself, and KPIs were highlighted as a tool for attaining this. KPIs are often seen as providing high-level snapshots of business performance. In reality, operational-level targets (KPIs you would set and/or try to achieve) are simply sub-set objectives of company wide KPIs that in turn relate to company performance objectives.

Measures typically consist of specific predefined measures (mostly quantitative) and may refer to reports, spreadsheets or charts, such as sales figures and trends over time, personnel- or employee-related statistics, supply chain information and so on. Significantly, they refer to any critical area of the business that is related to any of the business resources – time, people, money and use of space. Sir John Egan challenged the industry to achieve annual reductions of 10 per cent in costs and 20 per cent in defects – is this ambitious or simply stretching?

A major survey commissioned by the Confederation of British Industry (CBI) and *Building* Magazine suggested that overall construction performance had only increased by just over 10 per cent between 1995 and 1999. Nonetheless, it is hoped that the use of KPIs and benchmarking will help the industry move towards the kind of performance improvement desired by Egan.

High-level or macro performance indicators

High-level or macro performance indicators used in the construction industry and, in particular, the materials published by Constructing Excellence for use by managers are well advanced. You are advised to have a look at the various performance indicator toolkits available (see www.constructingexcellence.org.uk). They cover an extensive range including:

- *The working environment toolkit*: a checklist and scorecard which looks at staffing, recruiting and dealing with new employees, working conditions, welfare facilities and internal communications.
- *Equality and diversity in the workplace toolkit*: a checklist covering policy, recruitment and promotion, issues such as harassment and maternity leave, and monitoring employee satisfaction.
- *Health and Safety toolkits*: useful checklists covering client involvement during the construction phase, exposure to hazardous substances, muscular-skeletal hazards, noise and vibration and so on.

In developing KPIs for your people, you would start by identifying specific target areas to monitor performance. As mentioned, these targets are likely to be a sub-set of a bigger company-wide target. For example, site maintenance costs would be an element of overall building costs. Whatever your managerial level, KPIs can be predefined and provide you with information that you need to assess employee actions. For example, if the goal of the manager or supervisor is to improve customer satisfaction, then several KPIs could be formed and monitored to assess performance. What measures should you use? I divide the measures I use into two distinct, but clearly connected, areas. First, there are what I call my 'business' targets. These commonly relate to my responsibilities as part of the overall purpose of the firm and usually include measures to manage money and physical resources – plant, machinery and the like – and those related to providing service to customers – internal as well as external.

The Department of Trade and Industry (DTI) monitors the performance of the construction and provides KPIs that come with industry average performance. They can be used as project and company KPIs. For example, the figures assist companies in benchmarking their current and, perhaps, desired performance targets. Table 4.1 provides some detail.

Project KPIs	Definition	Scale	Industry average
Client satisfaction – product	How satisfied the client was with the finished product/facility	1–10	8
Client satisfaction – service	How satisfied the client was with the service	1–10	8
Defects	The condition of the product/facility at handover	1–10	8
Predictability – design cost	The actual cost less estimated cost expressed as a percentage	as %	0–14% *
– construction cost	The actual cost less the stated cost at 'commit to construct'	as %	0%
– construction time	Actual duration at 'available for use' less estimated duration at 'commit to construct'	as %	0%
Profitability	Company profit before tax and interest as percentage of sales	as %	4–6%
Productivity	Company value added per employee	£'s	28 000
Construction cost	Construction cost less the cost of a similar project one year earlier	as %	approx 3%
Safety	Reportable accidents per 100 000 employed per year	n=	2 236

* Depends on the benchmark for all construction, new-build housing, new-build non-housing, repair and maintenance (housing), repair and maintenance (non-housing).

Table 4.1 *The ten construction industry KPIs*

Source: DTI (2002).

The ten construction industry KPIs are updated each year to allow construction enterprises to benchmark their performance with that currently achieved in the industry. The indicators also allow contractors and consultants to demonstrate to prospective clients how results compare with competitors within the construction sector. They provide a clear and simple demonstration of how the firm is improving over time. Some examples of improvement might include:

- *Cost predictability*: a 20 per cent year-on-year improvement.
- *Construction cost*: a year-on-year improvement in cost efficiency.
- *Construction time*: a year-on-year improvement in time efficiency.
- *Defects*: a 20 per cent year-on-year reduction in defects.
- *Safety*: a reduction in accidents by 20 per cent per year.

An improvement in profitability is clearly a company target that may result from the above operational improvements. However, it will probably not be something that is normally disclosed to prospective clients. Nevertheless, as an example, a company may aspire to an increase in turnover and profit of, say, 10 per cent year-on-year.

Your more specific targets will probably be similar to the above, especially those that are budget-related cost measures. You will be responsible for continually meeting your allocated/agreed budget targets on a short-term basis. It is likely therefore that you receive a month-end report that shows your budgeted costs against what you have actually spent. The report is also likely to show the variance in both money terms and percentage terms, illustrating the difference between budgeted and actual costs. It is your job to be able to explain positive or negative variances and be able to answer the question 'Why did they vary?'.

You and your people may also be measured on your ability to increase the general effectiveness of the operations of your unit. This probably includes such performance targets as productive efficiencies, quality of product, meeting production schedules on time, minimizing expenses, reducing customer complaints, dealing with enquiries within a certain time period and so on. Of course, if you use only conventional quantitative performance measures such as looking at revenues, expenses, profit, cost variances and output, it is likely that short-run economic gains may be at the expense of long-run goals or the firm's strategic objectives. It will be clear that employees can add or take away value from any or all of the above measures. Of particular interest would be the industry averages for employee productivity and safety figures – improving the productivity per employee figure also improves company profit.

Process/people targets

People can be performance accumulators or denominators.

After reading Chapter 2, it should be clear that gaining commitment from people provides for high performance outcomes. Failure to appreciate people who are responsible for activities will adversely affect employee morale, loyalty, trust, motivation and overall commitment to the company. Consequently, I call my second category of measures 'process/people targets'.

In support of the vital recruitment, retention and respect for people agenda, the Movement for Innovation (M4I) working group report incorporated toolkits to monitor performance and improve key aspects of performance. Some have already been mentioned. They now also include career development, lifelong learning and, of course, worker satisfaction. Generally, these toolkits highlight 'respect for people' and carry detailed KPIs (sometimes referred to in construction as PPIs – people performance indicators). These include:

- **Employee satisfaction**. How satisfied direct employees are with:
    - the amount of influence they have over their jobs
    - the amount of pay they receive
    - the sense of achievement they get from their work
    - the respect they get from their line managers/supervisors.

- **Staff turnover**. The number of direct employees that have left and been replaced, expressed as a percentage of the average number of direct employees per year.

- **Sickness absence**. The number of working days lost due to sickness per direct employee per year, expressed as the percentage of the total number of employee working days.

- **Safety at work**. Reportable accidents per 100 000 employed per year (that is, accident incidents rate).

- **Working hours**. The number of usual hours worked per week per direct employee in his/her main job.

- **Travelling time**. The number of minutes spent travelling on the single journey from home to work each day per direct employee.

- **Training**. The number of training days (on- and off-the-job) provided per employee per year, expressed as the percentage of the total number of employee working days per year.

- **Pay**. The gross weekly earnings (before tax) per full-time direct employee.

- **Investors in People**. The percentage of the direct employees covered by the Investors in People recognition. There are three stages in the IiP accreditation process:

- not involved
- formally committed to achieving
- a recognized Investor in People.

Note: The KPI only assesses the final stage.

Table 4.2 indicates industry performance measures recorded by the DTI.

Respect for People KPIs	Measure	2001
Employee satisfaction	% scoring 8/10 or better	33%
Staff turnover	Median staff turnover (%)	9%
Sickness absence	Median sickness absence (days)	4
Safety (all employees)	Mean accident incident rate/100k employed	1849
Safety (companies > £10m)	Mean accident incident rate/100k employed	2236
Working hours	Median usual hours worked per week	44
Travelling time	Median travel time to work (mins)	31
Training	Mean annual training days (full-time staff)	3
Pay	Mean gross weekly earnings (£)	365
Investors in People	% workforce covered by IiP recognition	15.4%

Source: DTI (2002, pp. 226–31).

ONLY one-third of employees are 80 per cent or more satisfied at work.

Table 4.2 *Summary of industry performance – 'Respect for People' KPIs – 2001*

I'd like to make a few general comments about the DTI measures and results. First, they are key parameters that most companies can easily generate from personnel records. If records are not available, you have to create and monitor your own. For instance, as a simple but typical example of recording each person's absence, have a look at Figure 4.1.

Second, all KPIs are based and/or might be perceived on assumptions that may not always apply. For example, do longer travelling times to work affect employee performance? If you increase training days will it improve performance? Should a high staff turnover be avoided? Much clearer is the view that accidents must be minimized. Setting aside the legal and moral need for all to be responsible for the safety of others, around 2 per cent of the workforce affected by accidents in work cannot be regarded as a good use of people. It is also clear that poor pay dissatisfies employees. Importantly, it is also generally accepted that employee satisfaction with their job, their management, their working conditions and their colleagues, as well as a lack of general recognition, affects employee performance.

Monthly and Annual Summary of Absence				
Year:	Manager:		Department/Site/Location:	
Given name:			Family name:	
Hours of absence and reason for absence				
Month	Sickness or accident		Other absence		Reason for 'unauthorized' absence
	Certified	Uncertified	Authorized	Unauthorized	
January					
February					
March					
April					
May					
June					
July					
August					
September					
October					
November					
December					
Total for year					

Figure 4.1 *Sample monthly and annual summary of absence form*

Based on the DTI figures, we might state that only one-third of the employees surveyed were either satisfied or very satisfied as to the influence they have over their own jobs, the amount of pay they receive and the respect they get from their line manager. What about the other two-thirds? What commitment do they show? What is the effect on company performance? It does not take an Einstein to project that most companies suffer from levels of sub-optimal employee motivation and commitment.

Walter Llewellyn and Sons Ltd are mentioned in the *Respect for People: A Framework for Action* report (Respect for People, 2003a). PPIs in this company have provided an insight to the softer issues. Whilst recognizing that some people-related measures are very hard to measure, they have learnt not to take all results at face value – seeking to find root causes (not just performance-related symptoms) can be very enlightening.

I have completed research that broadened the categories related to employee performance and enabled the construction of a priority list of issues affecting employee commitment. These are:

1 poor or inappropriate human resource policies and practices
2 incoherent company and employee values
3 the structure of the work itself
4 confidence in senior management
5 general lack of recognition

6   poor consideration of employees by senior management
7   lack of advancement
8   too little or too much empowerment
9   poor working conditions
10 lack of immediate manager support
11 poor pay (as perceived by the employee against fair pay for the job they do)
12 lack of contact with senior management
13 lack of, or too much, responsibility
14 poor peer relationships
15 thwarting an employee's need for achievement.

It seems like general common sense that if employees do not feel recognized, empowered and satisfied with their work and working conditions, they are likely to be less committed to their organization. Employee satisfaction surveys that measure the above aspects are now commonplace in organizations in all industry sectors, regardless of whether they are private, public or non-profit. Ongoing support can be obtained following the *Respect for People: A Framework for Action* report. Industry-wide measures include questionnaires about workforce satisfaction, satisfaction surveys and charts all of which provide you with a chance to benchmark your survey results against those of other firms.

My own research work includes two further surveys:

1   A *General Satisfaction Survey* (GSS). This survey is based on field research related to what motivates people.

2   An *Employee Commitment Survey* (ECS). This survey is used extensively for research purposes and provides average levels of employee commitment by team, department, division and so on.

Questionnaires that help measure employee satisfaction and commitment.

Companies (small, medium or large) who are interested in assisting this research should contact me at d.j.cooper@salford.ac.uk

Benchmarking

Benchmarking is simply a method of improving performance in a systematic and logical way by measuring and comparing your firm's, your team's or your own activities as a manager against others, and then using the lessons learned from the best to design, instigate and implement improvements. Benchmarking is not a method of finding out the average performance and keeping to it. The benchmark you aim for is to provide 'best in class' performance – you and your firm should strive to be, or hold, the benchmark. To achieve 'best in class', you first need to be able to answer six questions:

1 Which performance measures need to be improved?
2 Are my measures reliable?
3 Who performs better?
4 Why do they perform better?
5 Are my people ready and willing to improve?
6 What actions do I/we need to take in order to improve my own and/or my team/section/department/function/site and company's performance?

As the first question suggests, you need to establish what needs to be improved. You also need to carefully select measures by which benchmark monitoring can take place – previous sections of this chapter should assist. Key aspects will be those that directly or indirectly affect customers.

The most obvious benchmark to use is past performance on selected KPIs against current performance. An internal benchmarking focus is also easily established. This is where you compare internal operations such as one site or project team against another site or project team in the same company.

Suites of KPIs are published nationally, so you can benchmark your people's performance against national performance ratings. In addition, use any organization or target that you see as the best. However, when choosing a target, make sure it is similar in structure to the one you or your company is using. It is also best to benchmark similar organizations in the same industry, in similar marketplaces, of a similar size and, if possible, working in a similar locality – for instance, you might make comparisons against a specific competitor for the same product, service or activity. Such an approach provides not only more meaningful and focused targets for improvement, but also data and more general information (not necessarily always quantitative) about what competitors are achieving. You may wish to join a local or regional 'benchmarking club' or network to aid this process.

If you are a manager in a small- to medium-sized construction enterprise (SMEs), it is worth mentioning that the DTI's Small Business Service, with support from the Construction Best Practice Programme, has developed a benchmarking index for SMEs to compare their performance against other firms. The index is now the largest collection of SME performance data in Europe. Contact can be made via www.benchmarkindex.com

You then need to determine the current performance gap. This is the difference between the best example benchmark and your current performance. For me, this is an ongoing exercise, so let me give you a brief example. I currently benchmark my own faculty (five higher education schools brought together under one management team) against the performance of other faculties in my university. I use measures not dissimilar to most firms. They include total income and income from each product and service. I measure employee costs, administration costs and review overheads (or indirect costs).

I also look at measures related to productivity – for example, how many students I have per academic staff member, non-employment costs per staff member, staff turnover, working conditions such as space per staff member, as well as facilities per student and staff member. I won't go on, but hopefully this gives you some idea. I then benchmark these KPIs. This is achieved by simply comparing my faculty's KPI results against other faculties' KPI results. I also compare my results against the results from the same KPIs in the same quarter of previous years. Let me add that, before I jump to conclusions about performance gaps, I make sure that all faculties categorize, measure and record similar KPIs in the same way. This may be an obvious point to make, but it is important nonetheless. The benchmarking process collapses – indeed, it would be better not to benchmark at all – if the measures are all formed in a different way. The results would not be worth having. More importantly, if I acted on the information that such a false comparison gave me, I could end up making interventions (with all good intention) that might inevitably damage performance.

If I have confidence in my benchmarking process, I then think about why performance gaps exist. Of course, gaps can be positive, in which case they point to areas where you, your team or your company hold the 'high ground'. Nevertheless, in my experience, there are always a few annoying negative gaps in performance and you have to work to 'plug them up' with a view to turning these 'problematic KPIs' into a strength.

Monitor, Evaluate and **Use** benchmarked results!

There is little point in producing and agreeing performance measures if you do not monitor and evaluate them. They must be continuously reviewed. You might wish to chart progress and display them in a prominent position so that your people can see their unit's performance at a glance. For some of my people, I also provide additional budget and performance reports. Of course, you should use the conventional appraisal or personal/personnel review system. This is a crucial part of the performance management process and involves a quarterly or annual event and formal review that allows you to discuss past performance on KPI targets and results with individual members of your staff. Appraisals are covered later in this chapter.

Measure both the new performance and the effect of any interventions deemed necessary and adjust as appropriate. Remember that making plans to improve performance is not good enough. You must ensure there is an appropriate level of ability and willingness from your people to change and adapt so that performance can improve. Finally, carry on repeating the process – by their nature, continuous improvements do not stop! Benchmarking only works well if you persist with the measurements and communicate effectively to those responsible for improvements – up, down and across the company. Your next task is to work (perhaps with your team) on designing and then making interventions that should improve current performance. You collect ideas, make plans, coordinate and implement changes, then monitor results – a continuous cycle.

Some additional advice:

- Do not try to benchmark too many things. Select a few key areas and gradually add, take away or alter as dictated by the learning process.
- Concentrate on measures that really add value and are not just personal preferences or flavours of the month.
- Make sure that you are comparing like with like, and be precise – comparing 'apples with oranges' or failing to check for inaccurate measurement can be worse than no measurement at all.
- Don't change the measures too frequently. If you must alter them or add a few more, communicate the change to all interested parties and explain why measures need to change and what the purpose is of each measure.
- Feed back results in a way that will be understood by the receiver of the communication – you may need to use different methods for different people.
- Ask people what they think of the results and whether they have any ideas on how they could be improved.
- Involve people in ideas, ways and activities needed to improve performance. Remember the motivational effect of being involved.

Individual behavioural performance

Most of the measures mentioned above have a quantitative feel. So what about behavioural performance? You may recall that in Chapter 1, I mentioned the use of competency frameworks. If you assemble these frameworks correctly, the content will be measurable, even if it is more qualitative than quantitative. These frameworks (sometimes called competency maps) can be used to review your own and your people's behaviour. Working with behaviour can be very emotive, so I limit benchmarking to working with an individual member of staff. Compare previously agreed behavioural performance improvements against observed behaviour over the last agreed time period – say, 3–12 months. You could carry out this process as part of the appraisal review, but, experience has taught me that reviewing behavioural competency is best done in a less formal, but equally confidential, setting.

To help you in this process, when setting behavioural competency *measures* with someone, try using such questions as:

1 If this part of your job was done effectively, what would it look like?
2 Can you think of any ways in which the task might not be done well?

3 Can we agree on the sort of behaviour that, if done well, would produce good or poor results?

Agree and then write down the two sorts of behaviour.

When reviewing behavioural competence *performance,* ask questions such as:

1 Do you think this part of your job was done well?
2 What behaviours assisted good performance?
3 What behaviours might have adversely affected performance?

Do not refer to the person – focus on the activity. DON'T GET 'PERSONAL'.

If necessary, revert or return to the first three competency measure questions.

Clearly, working to improve behaviour is the hardest task of being a manager. It requires great skill but, if done correctly, can provide the most startling performance improvements. I have found that if I can get people to agree about someone we both know – who we both respect as a high-performing individual – that 'other' person becomes the behavioural benchmark. Referring to a third party in this way often makes discussion easier.

You will find that as discussion about behavioural competence becomes a regular event and trust between you and each member of your staff improves, the process can be made easier by building in a discussion and agreement relating to behavioural competency into the normal appraisal process.

The manager as appraiser

Let's face it, it is seldom that we look forward to someone assessing/appraising us or our work. It is often difficult to realize that assessment and evaluation of what we do is an essential process, whether what is being appraised is a new building we designed, a new bathroom we fitted, a new road we laid, a timber frame we constructed, or the way we deal with others around us. The prime reason why we normally don't like being appraised is that we are likely to take as a personal criticism anything that we perceive as being negative – such a reaction is not helpful but is only human. As managers, we cannot ignore the use of appraisal as an important part of the performance management process, but we do need to employ good practice and techniques so that the result or outcome of the appraisal process is positive rather than negative.

The basis of appraisal – sometimes called performance review – is as follows:

1 Measurement: assessing results against agreed targets and standards.
2 Feedback: giving people information on how you think they are doing.
3 Positive reinforcement: emphasizing what has been done well.

4   Exchange of views: a discussion that should involve a full, free and frank exchange.
5   Agreement.

It is possible that your appraisal system involves ratings and is linked to individual performance-related pay. There are arguments for and against doing so – please refer to Chapter 2 for detail.

Performance reviews/appraisals are concerned with two parties getting together to engage in dialogue about performance and development. The process involves agreed assessment, an open exchange of views, feedback, positive reinforcement, an assessment of manager support, a discussion as to future support, and agreement as to future work and personal development plans. It is not something *done to* an individual; it is something that you and your people *carry out together* on a one-to-one basis. In terms of documentation that assists discussion about development, a personal development record such as the one shown in Figure 4.2 may be all that is required to help develop and monitor learning. Additional consideration is given to the training and development process later in this chapter.

From the employee's perspective, appraisals/performance reviews might provide them with an opportunity to state their views, to gain an improved understanding of important work measures and objectives, to provide a few new ideas and to obtain feedback on their past performance.

Unfortunately, many employee appraisals seem to result in worse manager-employee relationships. Cynically, some observers comment that it takes a whole year for the appraised to 'get over' the effects of the previous appraisal. Can you recall an appraisal that had a similar effect? For instance, you go into the appraisal/review meeting feeling nervous, feeling you have done a good job but still wondering whether your work has 'come up to scratch', worrying whether you will receive too much negative feedback that might undermine your self-esteem. During the review, you realize that most of the talking was done by your manager who is saying how performance must be improved and is totally ignoring issues like your need for development or training, or to discuss your career or how the firm might improve your working conditions. After the meeting you have mixed feelings.

On the one hand, you are glad that the process is over until next year. On the other hand, you feel frustrated that you did not get a chance to say what you really wanted to say and hear what you wanted to hear.

Sheet __ of __

Personal Development Record

To be updated prior to, and following, every learning experience. Please keep this form in your personal appraisal folder as part of your personal development plan.

Name:

Location:

Date of learning event	Pre-event learning objectives (Write down your objectives for the coming event)	Development/learning experience (Describe the learning event, what you did and what you learnt)	Post-event learning objectives (Write down learning objectives not met)	How will the learning be used? (Detail what you will do differently and how it will affect the team, company, etc.)	Date of next manager review of this learning	Comments/other learning required (Note anything you wish to bring to the attention of your manager, including additional learning required and how it might be obtained)

Figure 4.2 *Sample personal development record*

When you are appraising your people, you may wish to avoid some or all of the following – they can ruin the appraisal interview/process:

- *The halo effect and personal biases.* This occurs when you rate an employee very high or very low on the basis of one or just a few characteristics. You may have heard or experienced what to you is favouritism – the boss just seems to favour someone on the basis that they are pleasant, or perhaps support the same football team. Similarly, I have known managers to take an instant dislike to certain people. They allow themselves to be influenced by single characteristics, some of which do not sit well within the working environment. Sounds far-fetched? Well no! Managers may not be aware of acting favourably towards some people, but they do so, all the same. My only advice is to try to maintain an equal professional distance from, or closeness to, all of your employees. This is especially important for those immediately reporting to you – your team. Having or showing favouritism towards some, but not all, your team members can destroy it. Stay objective and value people on the basis of their overall performance.
- *Different standards.* This sounds similar to the halo effect but is very different. It occurs when two or more managers use different standards to assess their people who are doing the same job in similar circumstances. You may be surprised to learn that your people will talk to other people about what their manager says, what their job is like, what they are paid and so on. It won't be long before inconsistencies are discovered. If they are – and especially if different standards directly affect pay – just wait for the storm to occur.
- *Bringing up the past.* Remember that you are assessing performance over a given and agreed period of time – usually 12 months. Try not to let performance in bygone years/periods affect your judgement or very recent good performance colour your thinking. For example, I have known people who, knowing that their appraisal was about to occur, suddenly have a brief spurt of outstanding performance causing people who have performed consistently well over the full period to be overshadowed and treated unfairly as a result.

The good news for appraisers is that the appraisal process can work well. If you can develop adequate skills, provide a good environment for the meeting and discuss all areas related to an individual's performance, the process can probably provide an opportunity for meaningful dialogue and perhaps positively influence both parties' perceptions.

As part of the performance management process, it is essential, prior to the appraisal/review meeting, to ask the employee about his or her thoughts about their job, what they believe are the objectives of their job, and how both the job and the objectives might be improved. Send a preparation form to each employee about two or three weeks before the review meeting (see Figure 4.3).

You also need to prepare for the review meeting. If your company does not have a standard form, think about using something along the lines of Figure 4.4.

When conducting the review meeting, think about and apply the following guidelines:

- Allow the reviewed (sometimes referred to as the appraised or appraisee) to do the most talking.
- Listen actively – show you are listening and make a few notes.
- Concentrate on analysing performance – not personality.
- Recognize achievements and strengths.
- Always end the meeting positively.

'Knowledge speaks, but wisdom listens.' (Jimi Hendrix)

Although the appraisee should do most of the talking, remember that goals direct performance, but performance can only be maintained via accurate and timely feedback. The law of effect is a basic principle of learning stating that 'learning is controlled by its consequences'; this simply means that, without knowledge of consequences, learning cannot take place. Reviewing and feeding back information about their performance to people during the appraisal is vital to a process of continuous improvement.

You may think you have a good memory, but don't rely on it. Make notes about what has been discussed at the review meeting, and, importantly, on what has been agreed. A separate form is recommended – something along the lines of Figure 4.5.

Note that I have deleted many of the lines on all the forms, including that in Figure 4.5, to save space. Clearly, the form must be flexible to cater for as many objectives, plans and comments as you feel are necessary. If possible, try using electronic means (e-mail) to send and receive completed forms – but remember the need for confidentiality. E-mailing has revolutionized interoffice communication, but I find the system notorious for making it too easy to pass private information around to other people. At the very least, mark the communication private and confidential.

My only other comment is try to keep items such as objectives and plans to the most important ones. You and the job-holder should be able to remember the important measures and objectives without referring too frequently to the form itself.

Performance Management Review: Personal Preparation	
Name:	Job title:
Department:	Date:

1 In preparation for your review, list what you consider to be the important tasks of your job.

2 Write down what you believe are the main things you are trying to achieve (your objectives) in carrying out your job.

3 Write down your main achievements since your last review.

4 Have you met any problems in carrying out your work?
   If so, what sort of problems?
   What do you think could be done about them?

5 Do you believe that best use is being made of your skills and abilities?
   If not, what needs to be done?

6 Do you get satisfaction from your work? If so, what gives you the most satisfaction?
   If not, what prevents you from being satisfied with your work?

7 Where would you like to go from here, i.e. your career, extra responsibilities, personal development, work aspirations?

Figure 4.3 *Sample performance management personal preparation form*

Performance Management Review: Manager's Preparation	
Name of job-holder to be assessed:	Job title:
Name of manager/reviewer:	Date:

1	What are the key tasks of the job-holder which you want to discuss?
2	List the objectives you would like to discuss with the job-holder with regard to each of the key tasks.
3	Record here how the job-holder's achievements are or could be measured or assessed (KPI performance measures)
4	Consider the results of measures that the job-holder achieved since the last review meeting. Note any where performance was particularly high and low. Can you think of any reason for the negative or positive variance in performance?
5	Are you content that the job-holder makes best use of his or her knowledge and skills? How might they be better used?
6	What do you think best motivates the job-holder, and do you think he or she is satisfied that work motivations are or could be fulfilled?
7	Note here what you think is the potential of the job-holder in terms of extra responsibility, career progression.
8	Does the job-holder need additional training and/or development in order to achieve current work performance or promotion?

Figure 4.4 *Sample performance management manager's preparation form*

Performance Management Review – Record	
Job-holder:	Department:
Manager/reviewer:	Period of review: From: To:

Achievement of objectives
(Comment on whether objectives were achieved, partly achieved or not achieved and the factors which are agreed to have affected performance)

Objectives	Achievements	Factors affecting

Action plans (what you decided to do)
(Comment on progress made in completing agreed action plans)

Action Plans	Achievements	Factors affecting

Training and development
(Comment on development and training received during the previous review period. How effective was it?)

Performance agreement for the period   From: To:

Agreed objectives	Agreed performance criteria
Agreed action plans	List how you both intend to accomplish the agreed action plans

Agreed development and training needs

Comments

Manager/reviewer	Signed:	Date:
Job-holder	Signed:	Date:
Manager's manager	Signed:	Date:

Figure 4.5 *Sample performance management review record form*

The appraisal process can also provide feedback to you, as appraiser, because it can help confirm employee perceptions as to management objectives, intentions and priority values. This is important because many managers receive very few honest comments about how their actions might affect others. After all, who wants to risk the possibility of the boss taking exception to opinions, despite their well-meaning and constructive nature? To overcome this potential problem, some firms have introduced a 360-degree appraisal/performance review process for managers. Such a scheme can be extended to all employees but, because it is time-consuming and therefore costly, it is often limited to middle and senior managers.

There are several different 360° feedback appraisal schemes. However, most that are in use in the construction industry offer you feedback from your immediate manager (or your immediate manager's boss). This may be informed via client feedback, your peers (people usually on the same pay scale/grade as you and working closely with you), other internal customers – for example, someone who relies on your work performance to do their job effectively – and your direct reports – your people. Such a scheme can provide you with an awareness of any discrepancy between how you see yourself and how others see you – from all directions. The process of receiving information about general performance (behaviour included) enhances your self-awareness and is critical for personal and professional development. Clearly, you need to be able to receive constructive criticism as well as praise. This is not always easy – I have seen it upset a few managers.

Although I have a few doubts about the 360° mechanism, nonetheless, as you obtain higher management responsibility, you would do well to realize that, in medium to large enterprises, most employees are disconnected from you by locality and/or job responsibilities. The 360° scheme can provide you with vital information which otherwise might have been filtered on its way to you.

One extra value from the appraisal process that is often overlooked, therefore, is that it ensures, and perhaps enforces, personal contact between you and your people. Generally speaking, contact with people is important. This seems especially so in industries like construction where the successful completion of projects relies on many people who do not always have the opportunity to work closely on a day-to-day basis. Nevertheless, good managers argue that good communication between them and their people should be a natural occurrence. In many ways, appraisals are often used by firms as a 'stop-gap' simply because many managers do not (or do not have sufficient time to) communicate well. Companies also know that, without appropriate communication, you and the firm will miss out on some innovative ideas, important information, getting agreement about objectives and so on. The general rule is that you need to find more ways of ensuring adequate contact with people over and above the appraisal process. This is especially important for middle and senior managers (refer back to 'Communication' in Chapter 3).

Training and developing your people and your personal development

Training and developing your people

This section looks at training and development. Training, education and development are simply approaches to improving and supporting people to learn new knowledge, skills and attitudes in order to improve their performance. There are several means of enabling learning, including on-the-job training, off-the-job training, personal self-development, management development, vocational training, further education, higher education, lifelong learning and professional development, amongst others.

The use of learning contracts is a useful way of getting people's agreement about the learning that they need.

As a manager you have your limitations – you cannot make people learn. Your job is to understand what learning each of your people requires in order to improve their performance. However, I have found the use of learning contracts a useful way of getting people's agreement about the learning that they need. A sample learning contract is shown in Figure 4.6.

I should state that your goal as manager is to encourage competence from learning in order to improve people's performance. Training and developing people is an important means to that end. Competence was introduced in Chapter 1; to reiterate, it is thought that raising levels of competence:

1 helps to attract higher-quality employees
2 improves business performance (improves individual, team and corporate performance)
3 enables better matching of people to jobs
4 provides a common language for managers to assess improvements
5 makes better use of (always finite) training resources
6 helps minimize learning costs
7 assists in focusing people development activities
8 makes for improved and objective performance reviews
9 provides for flexible multiskilled employees
10 helps identify transferable skills (from one job to another).

As a practitioner whose job was to help educate, train and develop people, I always found it easier to try and separate education, training and development into different processes and activities – it simply helped me prescribe the best and most cost-effective form of learning for each person, team, department and so on. However, it is worth remembering that each process enables learning with the intention of improving competence to aid performance.

Learning Contract	
Name:	**Job title:** **Location:**

Goal *(What you intend to learn and why)*

Learning *(What knowledge or skills will be acquired)*

Plan *(How are you going to achieve your goal? Specify training courses or development, on- or off-the-job, education, project work, etc.)*

Resources *(How much time or help from your manager will be required? Do you need any other resources?)*

Outcomes *(What learning will occur? How will it affect your skills, knowledge and/or behaviour? How will the outcomes be measured?)*

Signed:	**Date:**
Signed (manager):	**Date:**

Figure 4.6 *Sample learning contract*

'Education is a progressive discovery of our own ignorance.' (Will Durant)

It is fair to say that the borderline between training, development and education is often blurred. Nevertheless, education usually refers to learning that takes place in a structured and formal way and forms part of an institutional 'taught' programme, such as a GNVQ, HNC, HND, BSc, MBA or MSc. Training can have obvious links with vocational learning. However, it may best be viewed as a planned process to improve your people's job-related knowledge and skills. It is more immediate and usually more easily arranged than education or longer-term development. An example of a training event might be a one day off-the-job training course to learn, and perhaps practise, a new technique to fit UPVC windows or a new computer system to design kitchens. The advantage of training is clear; it assists the development of skills, provides knowledge and skills to help manage change, improves communication and helps develop a positive and progressive organizational culture.

Training is also an important aspect of 'Respect for People' and contributes to performance and retention. The CITB states categorically that the competitiveness of the construction sector is underpinned by a skilled and qualified workforce – a workforce that is able to meet the challenges of today as well as cope with the technologies of tomorrow. To this end, the CITB has created a wide range of course materials and provides National and Scottish Vocational Qualification programmes that cover technical, supervisory and management training. Interested readers should contact the CITB customer service team (see 'Useful Addresses' at the end of this book).

Development may include training events but is more concerned with providing plans and activities for ongoing 'total learning' designed to meet the future development needs of an individual – it is often perceived as being costly and time-consuming and may therefore become reserved (wrongly in my view) for management and people of 'management potential'.

It is not uncommon for firms to separate training and development and talk of 'employee training' and 'management development'. For example, you might wish to put on a training event through which people can receive information about controlling costs. This might be useful for all employees. However, for people who will have responsibility for monitoring and controlling costs, you may produce a development plan whereby they attend a training course, have a short secondment in finance, work on a project with a management accountant, produce a format for future cost reports and so on. Notice that 'development' normally involves a series of activities designed to improve skills, knowledge and attitudes that assist in improving people's future performance.

From experience, I prefer the use of development activities in support of technical, supervisory and management training and education. You will also find that designing development

(development plans) using on-the-job development activities can prove to be a very cost-effective way of steadily improving people's performance. More importantly, development plans help ensure that newly acquired skills are immediately used to good advantage within the workplace.

Below are two comments I overheard about training people:

- *'Over half of UK firms do not give training to managers.'* Which half of the UK does your company fit?

- *'The UK not only suffers from insufficient training but also inefficient and ineffective training at all levels of the organization.'* How do you rate the training you have been given or your people have experienced? If it was less than useful, why do you think that happened? How might it have been improved? If you can recall a training event being very useful, write down why it was so effective. What responsibility should you take to ensure training is both cost- and work performance-effective?

Conventionally, planned training goes through a standard process. I have altered the normal process to include development. Importantly, managers can take an active interest in all the steps. Here they are:

1 Identify training needs.
2 List well-defined learning requirements.
3 Decide whether a training or development approach is best for each learning requirement.
4 Plan training and/or development activities/events/ programmes.
5 Decide on techniques, facilities, locations and trainers.
6 Implement training and development.
7 Evaluate training, development and learning.

When I was a management training and development manager of a multinational organization, I formulated a slight variance to the above steps and gave the process a far more practical feel. I have recommended this approach to several construction firms:

1 Identify major training and development needs. Think about impending changes in the company's strategy, organizational changes, new structures, machinery, staff deployment and so on.
2 Agree with other managers possible solutions to the perceived training and development gap. In my experience, in order to meet the organization's three- to five-year strategic intent, there is normally a gap between where its functions, departments, sections and individuals are right now compared with where they would, or should, be in the future. Given a magic wand, what changes are desired?

'The best way to predict the future is to invent it.'
(Alan Kay)

3   Select training and development options. Nothing new here. Use on- and off-the-job methods, consultants, in-house trainers /line managers and so on. However, focus should be heavily weighted on development activities – such as allocating project work, job enhancements, work rotation, team development, mentoring, pilot schemes, think tanks, coaching and so on – rather than on training. Development activities can work out more cost effective than training, they are usually more closely related to work activity and they normally occur in or around the working environment. Consequently, managers have greater control and influence over the learning that comes from them and, as a result, they can be more closely matched to operational objectives. In many ways, knowledge and skills obtained through development activities are more easily transferred into the working environment.

4   Create a training and development plan for each part of the company – right down to subsections – and linked with individual appraisals/personnel reviews, and create personal development plans for each person. This is not as long-winded as it sounds. If you focus on key training and development needs, some plans will be quite small, forming a part of a more long-term aspiration for improvement.

5   Implement training and development activities/events/prog-rammes, but be sure to get managers at all levels to 'buy-in' to the plan and take an active part.

6   Evaluate – you cannot do enough of it. Try to look for quantifiable (usually financial benefits linked to better cost control or productivity) but also more intangible benefits. As a guide, use the following conventional five-level evaluation process:

– **Level 1:** *Reactions.* What do trainees think about the training and development they have experienced?

– **Level 2:** *Learning.* Have the trainees gained new knowledge and skills?

– **Level 3:** *Job behaviour.* This is usually based on line manager observations and/or work related statistics – how much transfer of learning from training to job can you observe? This is an exercise that is worth doing but can be seen as a little too qualitative (soft) for some managers.

– **Level 4:** *Organizational unit.* This evaluation is usually carried out by department heads or site managers – what improvements have occurred in output, productivity, quality and so on? Clearly, improvements should relate directly to agreed KPIs.

– **Level 5:** *Ultimate values.* Has the organization/firm benefited from the learning event(s)? This may involve collating the results from all of the first four levels and

'As I grow older, I pay less attention to what men say, I just watch what they do.' (Andrew Carnegie (1835–1919)).

chatting with senior management or the directors. It is really a question of gathering all information/data and applying senior-level judgement.

You should involve yourself in all five stages of evaluation. In this way, the overall benefits of the training plan and process have more of a chance of being transferred and used.

What about possible pitfalls?

1 Training and development must be aligned with organizational /departmental objectives. If it is not, it may be seen as a waste of valued and finite resources – for example, time and money. You have probably experienced training that does not connect at all with your job or future job. Perhaps not a complete waste of time – but close.
2 Let's face it, some off-the-job training is awful! If using external training providers, make sure that the design and delivery of the training is up to scratch. If using internal means, take an active part in the design. For example, make sure that you agree with the learning outcomes and check the content to see whether the individual can benefit from the experience.
3 If you do not have the full support of senior management, the merits of training and development or the fit with company objectives will possibly remain hidden. Try to make an appropriate and timely evaluation and make sure that senior managers know about improvements brought about by the process.
4 Line and middle managers must also be supportive. They are the people that ensure that the worth of training and dev-elopment is transferred into the job. If you or they are sceptical of the value, then little transference will occur. Quite simply, the benefits of the learning are lost or, perhaps worse, the knowledge and skills remain trapped in the head of the trainee/ participant until they leave your firm and move to your main competitor.
5 Try to ensure that trainees are motivated before, during and after the training/learning event. Provide pre- and post-training interviews, show interest and use the opportunity as a coaching session – focus on potential job improvements.
6 Finally, training and development cannot be optimized if the company has other people-related support systems, processes, procedures and practices that are inadvertently or deliberately designed to negate the worth of the training activity.

Let me provide further clarity on point 6. It is no good sending a trainee on a finance course if they will not be given responsibility to manage or contribute to the management of money. Don't send them on a creative thinking course if there isn't an innovation scheme, or they are simply told what to do and when to do it in their current working climate. A philosophy or work culture such as 'Get it right first time' will not fit very well with the chief executive's call to 'Be innovative, try out something new'. How about an empowerment programme for people who are asked to be accountable but who will not be given any delegated responsibility or authority? Or, what about requesting line managers to attend a cultural change programme with a view to organizational improvement without first checking the culture emanating from the boardroom? How about a teambuilding programme that emphasizes the need for team synergies for people whose salaries are totally based on individual performance-related pay? I could go on but, thankfully, I won't. It is perhaps needless to say, in such cases as these, that all that transpires is a frustrated employee, a clear cost to the organization and no measurable improvement in performance.

People studying at further and higher education institutes can greatly assist performance. Such study is particularly useful for people who wish to achieve and prepare themselves for higher-level positions within the firm. However, I think that some managers find managing people who are studying for high-level qualifications quite daunting. The only advice I can offer is to take an interest in what your people are studying and try your best to spot and support new ideas that could be useful to the company.

If you manage training, development and educational opportunities well, you can expect performance improvements. Clearly, you can take an active role in developing employee competence. You can and should develop your trainer skills and take part in training – perhaps making guest appearances during training events (some of these skills were covered in Chapter 3). A decision to use training specialists should result in an increase in knowledge. If you yourself take an active role, it seems likely that the training outcomes will also include a willingness to implement new-found knowledge and an increase in commitment. Quite simply, taking part in training helps develop the interface between manager and employee; it is an opportunity that no manager should miss.

Personal development

Management development may be a key objective of your firm and be observable via management training and development plans. These plans normally emanate from human resource plans that in turn relate to the organization's wish to achieve strategic objectives (mentioned in Chapter 3 as part of my explanation of strategic HRM). The reason for the plan may be to assist quality, cost reduction and profitability through individual, organizational and cultural change – or through all of these. Conversely, management training and development plans may have a definite purpose – for example, to extend the role of line and middle managers. Regardless of whether or not your firm has such plans, you hold a responsibility to develop yourself and your people.

First, try thinking about your own management and professional development:

- Consider your own learning needs. Try to anticipate what changes may occur within your working environment, your company, the construction industry. Rereading Chapter 1 may help.
- Consider your own career aspirations. Not all people at all points in their careers want to rise within the managerial ranks. However, if you do, what area and/or level of managerial work would you wish to achieve? What skills, knowledge and behavioural competency (discussed in Chapter 1) do you need to attain?
- Initiate self-learning. Find out (if you don't know already) how best you learn, then provide for yourself a simple learning plan and perhaps a Gantt chart showing how and when you will take part in training and/or development activities. Not a wish list – a to-do list!
- Execute your learning plan. It is best to let your company and those around you know what you are doing so that when, and if, support is needed, it can be called upon.
- Remember that, regardless of your preferred learning style, you will need time to reflect on, and evaluate, your learning. If you have a mentor, make sure that you use them. If you have a specialist human resource person, have a chat with them – their experience can be invaluable. Remember, a clever man learns from their mistakes, but a wise man also learns from other people's mistakes.

A wise man (person) also learns from other people's mistakes.

Investors in People (IiP)

In my view, training people is absolutely critical if you want or need improved performance. The popularity of the Investors in People scheme is due to the fact that many construction firms and leading bodies agree with the sentiment that you must invest in people because they are assets. The scheme gains mention as a recommended 'key success indicator' in the report *A Commitment to People – Our Biggest Asset* (Respect for People, 2003b) and is reinforced in *Accelerating Change* as central to the development of an enhanced 'people' culture. Peter Lobban, chief executive of the CITB categorically states that 'Investors in People has a vital role to play in helping construction companies, particularly the many SMEs, to improve their business performance through developing the skills of their employees' (CITB, 2003). The CITB also states that 'Our industry is increasingly characterized by regulation, by rising customer expectations, by increased competition and by a potential skills shortage' and goes on to suggest that:

> *The Investors in People standard is being used as a business development tool by thousands of organizations in all employment sectors across the UK. It was developed over 10*

years ago by the business community to make organisations more competitive, through effective communication, focused planning and action, and a commitment to continuous improvement throughout the workforce. (CITB, 2003).

Quoted business benefits include:

- more efficient use of resources
- direction given to the business
- workforce focused on the needs of customers (internal and external) and able to deal with them efficiently
- enhanced company image – gaining respect from customers and making it easier to recruit the best people
- focused training and development
- better communications.

Investors in People is a national standard that sets a level of good practice in terms of people development with a view to improving the firm's overall performance.

Companies wishing to achieve IiP accreditation and receive the coveted IiP award must ensure that:

- they are committed to investing in people to achieve business goals
- they demonstrate the planned development of people
- they provide evidence that developmental actions/interventions take place and that they are part of a continuing programme directly tied to business objectives
- the outcomes of training and development are evaluated in terms of their value to the individual and the organization.

It is also worth mentioning that the CITB may provide generous funding for training within the industry. Interested readers should contact the CITB at <www.citb.org.uk>. The organization also provides advice on, and templates for, the creation of individual and company training plans. In addition, the Rethinking Construction partners have provided a Training Plan Toolkit comprising training needs questionnaires and skills summary templates for plant operators, operative and craft workers and technical, supervisory and management personnel. The Toolkit is adapted from the CITB grant scheme model. Consequently, if your company is eligible for a CITB grant, it is recommended that you use their more detailed version.

In addition to providing for new knowledge and skill development, the process of training and developing people improves people commitment both to management and to the organization itself. It is therefore interesting that, given this connection, cutting training budgets is often a company's first reaction when performance outcomes appear to be threatened.

Clearly, everyone would accept the need for organizations to survive during difficult periods. Nonetheless, management should accept that cutting resources allocated for training and development not only affects employees' opportunities to apply newly acquired knowledge and skills for the betterment of the organization, but also their motivation and commitment. The converse is also true. Training and development is as much about employees feeling appreciated and considered by their management as it is a chance to develop themselves. Consequently, it is an important part of the motivation element of 'recognition' and can therefore be used by management as a means of showing consideration and helping to enhance commitment.

Dealing with performance problems

Managing the problem

However good a company's performance management processes are, and however well they are applied, and however well focused are the training and development interventions, problems will still arise from time to time. But what do we mean by performance problems and what can you, as manager do about them? Quite simply, you are faced with a performance problem when an individual or group can be identified as responsible for a shortfall against a desired performance or target – for instance, if you have established and agreed specific operational KPIs and an individual or group of people underperforms and fails to achieve the desired target. Your first step, in this case, is to identify and agree with those concerned the reason for the underperformance. You should also be aware of circumstances that may occur that are beyond your people's responsibility, authority or accountability. It is no good blaming individuals for weaknesses in systems, processes and market/price/cost fluctuations beyond their control – that's how grievances start. Some general steps as to how to approach performance problems may be of help:

Who owns this problem anyway?

1   Agree what the shortfall is in quantifiable and/or qualitative terms. This is much easier if you have agreed performance targets in place. If you have implemented a system with which the individual(s) concerned will have been able to monitor their performance automatically, then this stage of the problem process will be easier – after all, prevention is better than the need for a cure.
2   Establish the reason for the shortfall. So often we managers immediately seek to find someone who is responsible for the shortfall rather than seek the means to rectify the situation first – that's how blame cultures start!
3   Try to work towards managing the problem through agreement rather than blame. Identify all possible factors that have, or might have, contributed to the shortfall.

4 Isolate those factors beyond the control of the individual or group.

5 Identify any mitigating factors that affected performance – for example, poor or no training, incomplete understanding of what was expected, poor management, lack of, or poor, systems or process.

6 Isolate factors directly attributable to the individual or group – for example, an ability, skill or attitude shortfall.

7 Decide and agree what action is required to ensure the shortfall does not continue. Clarify expectations. For example, revisit the original job requirements, have a look at the job specification and personal specification and review the last appraisal/performance review documentation.

8 As appropriate, instigate training and development to improve knowledge, skill and/or change attitudes. However, be sure to make clear to the individual or group your expectations about the result and performance outcome from the process.

9 Put the plans into action. This may involve using your ability to apply training, coaching and perhaps even counselling skills (as discussed in Chapter 3). The only problem left is to choose the appropriate technique, approach and intervention for the prevailing circumstances. I use the chart depicted in Figure 4.7 to point me in the right direction. I hope you find it as useful as I have over the past 20 years.

10 As usual, no guide would be complete without stating the obvious. Ensure that appropriate measures are in place, then monitor and provide feedback as to whether there are improvements or no improvements in performance.

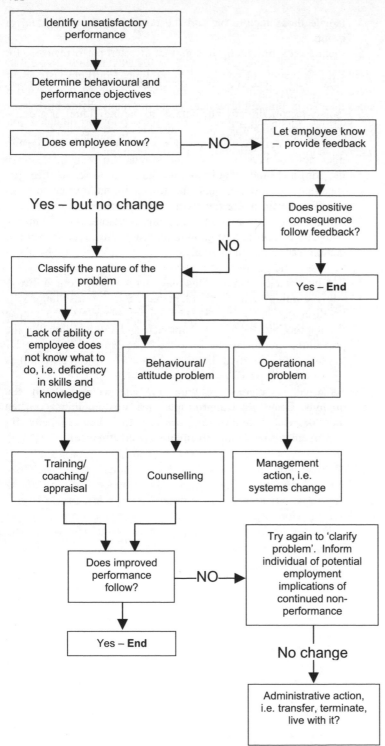

Figure 4.7 *Using training, coaching and counselling skills to deal with performance problems*

Managing conflict

It is unlikely that you will be able to manage without becoming involved in a dispute or conflict at some time. Conflict exists when there is a disagreement about a situation and where two or more sides take an incompatible stance. There are many different reasons for conflict, including personality clashes, poor or outdated job design, arguments over the distribution of resources, conflicting values and goals or perspectives, or even boredom.

Keep your head while all those around you are losing theirs – stay focused!

Most conflict situations can be resolved if those concerned can avoid making the original dispute worse by taking entrenched positions. What you, as manager, must avoid is taking the conflict personally, losing your temper, becoming autocratic and expecting the other party to apologize unconditionally. If any of this happens, the situation is already out of control.

People have different 'conflict styles'. Perhaps you try to accommodate other people with a view to maintaining good relationships. If this most closely matches the way you deal with conflict, you try to resolve the situation by adopting a technique that is unsurprisingly known as 'accommodating'. It consists of you taking a non-assertive and cooperative stance. This approach can be useful and may help maintain good relations.

Alternatively, you may 'dig your heels in' and try to solve the situation by insisting that you are right. This is a competitive stance; it is also aggressive and uncooperative. However, you may be surprised to hear that even this approach can have its uses. For example, it may be the correct response to conflict if you need quick and decisive action, and/or when you need to adopt an approach that you know others will not appreciate – for instance, the need to cut operating costs. Of course, the approach is only acceptable if you can explain why you have to take a competitive stance. If you cannot, you are in danger of losing valued commitment from your people. Moreover, it is not advisable to always take this stance.

Of course, you may decide to simply ignore the conflict situation. This approach involves being non-assertive, but also being uncooperative. It means that you ignore your own, as well as others' concerns, values, needs and so on. It may be a way of avoiding the conflict, delaying it, or hoping that someone else resolves it on your behalf. If the conflict is anything more than trivial (and most conflict situations are far more than trivial), this form of resolution is not recommended.

Out of the first three approaches to conflict, I most often use the accommodating technique to conflict resolution. However, I have a few important back-up approaches since it is possible to be overaccommodating, leading people to take advantage of your goodwill and/or good nature.

A fourth approach is to try compromising. The idea is to try to find a mutually acceptable middle ground by which both or all parties to the conflict can find a suitable, and perhaps face-saving, resolution. This is the 'give and take' technique so often used by firm but fair managers. Of course, you need to stay professional, keep your temper in check, look for ideas that are flexible, and agree solutions that solve the conflict without adversely affecting work operations.

As usual, I leave my preferred approach to the last. This is simply to maintain your assertive and cooperative behaviour while getting all parties to focus on the core problem or reason for the conflict. The idea is that you maintain a professional distance – that is, avoid aspects of the conflict that may take on a personal nature – aim for collaboration and get your people to work with you to find a solution. Clearly, this approach requires excellent interpersonal communication, questioning and feedback skills on your part while maintaining assertive behaviour (all described in Chapter 3).

It is said that, when you decide to adopt a collaborative approach to resolving conflict, you are simply recognizing that all parties have just cause to be concerned and that their views, needs, values and ideas both exist and are important. You may wish to reread parts of Chapter 2 about leadership. Although there will be times when adopting all five approaches to resolving conflict have their place, looking for collaboration can provide new ideas, better cooperation, improved teamwork, build trust, tap into individual and team motivations, and improve commitment and overall per-formance.

As you make your way through the above process ensure that you are familiar with various policy documents that assist improvement – for example, employment policies such as human resource planning, equality and diversity, health and safety, discipline, grievances and so on.

It is also worth remembering that, although you may wish not to take an entrenched stance, the other party may not be as professional in their outlook. In these situations, it is best to ensure that conversations and communications are vetted by your manager, personnel specialists or at least other colleagues. Disputes can get very nasty and lead to all kinds of legalized reviews and even tribunals. As a general guide, when I become aware of an impending conflict, I invite an independent person to monitor the situation. I also make concise but comprehensive notes about what has been said and by whom as soon as possible after each meeting, telephone call or other informal conversation.

To expect a business and working world without conflict would be naive. Chapter 2 illustrated the many different objectives, needs and aspirations that exist in all companies whatever their size. Where there are people, departments, teams and divisions with differing wants and motivations there will always be conflict. The measure of you, as a manager, is how you respond to these situations. It is always worth recalling that your job is to improve performance, so act in a way that is supportive of this end. In so doing, you will be able to maintain your integrity, keep natural frustrations 'out of harm's way' and, as a consequence, have a better chance of enabling a reasonable solution. You can then pat yourself on the back for a manager's job well done.

Summary

This chapter has considered the process of setting objectives, establishing important benchmarked measures, agreeing performance targets, and using them to monitor and assess performance. You may legitimately claim that you currently have insufficient time to manage your work responsibilities, but just imagine how difficult it would be without performance management methods to guide and help you!

The appraisal process was also discussed. It is worth remembering that the appraisal interview should review 'hard' or substantially quantitative measures, and 'soft' more qualitative performance areas. Both have their place, so aim for an acceptable and appropriate balance. There is more about the need for balance in Chapter 5.

Recall the question I asked you to consider in the introduction to this chapter: 'Do we use our performance process effectively?' Well, what do you think? Consider how you and your company/ section/team benchmark the service you give to clients/customers. Do you think that the measures you have in place accurately reflect your important responsibilities, activities and desired outcomes? Do your people performance measures 'measure up' to the needs of both the company and your people?

I hope the small section dedicated to managing problems and dealing with conflict will be useful. In my opinion, if there are going to be real problems at work they will most likely be people-related problems. One thing is certain: if you identify a problem and decide to leave it, it will very probably get worse.

We also looked at the important role of training and development for the company, for you as a developing manager, and for your people's overall performance and self-esteem. This brings me to the second question I suggested that you consider at the beginning of the chapter: 'Are my people being developed to their full potential in their existing jobs?' In your view, do company training plans accurately identify the most crucial areas requiring development? How useful is current training in your company, section or site? Can trainees immediately put their training to good use? Do you take time to talk with trainees before and after the training/learning event? Whether, as suggested in Chapter 3, you take an active part in training your people, or you feel others are best placed to provide training for you, remember that when evaluating training you must always be able to explain the benefits of training to both the company and the individual. Finally, don't forget your own need for continued professional development. The pace of change in construction demands that you keep your knowledge and skills up-to-date. After the developmental event, reflect on the learning experience, decide how it can be used effectively and consider whether you and the company would benefit from any further learning.

In the same way that each individual must continuously develop, so must the company. Consequently, the next and final chapter explains company-wide performance management models that assist continuous improvement.

Chapter 5

Future Strategies?

Your job is likely to be very broad and may include the need to manage money, physical resources, and other stakeholders such as suppliers, trade unions, customers, shareholders and/or other providers of finance, as well as managing people. Nevertheless, if your firm is providing good projects and/or services at the right time in the right place at the right price and at the right quality, it should be performing well. This means giving good returns on investment to owners and others who loan the company money and providing appropriate rewards, continuous employment and job satisfaction for people. It does not sound simple and, in practice, it definitely isn't simple. Although I understand and appreciate the idea of wanting to 'get it all right, first time and all the time', given the complexity of management, this demand often seems unreasonable. Nevertheless, I am absolutely convinced that if you manage people well, they will solve problems, make fewer mistakes, make use of opportunities and avoid threats to the business; in short, they will perform well and continuously improve.

Lessons for managers: pulling it all together

There is a growing acceptance that most of the variance between poor and high-performing companies is related to people and, in particular, to the way they are managed. Chapter 1 asserted that 'people are the organization's biggest asset'. This saying was once regarded as something that only human resource managers said in a plea for more senior figures to support them but nowadays research continuously supports this view with empirical evidence (as close to proof as research can get). The construction industry is undergoing a change that demands a different and vastly improved management process. You are challenged to develop your people's competencies and make good use of them through effective performance management systems and processes.

Chapter 2 described the importance of good management and the difference between management and good leadership. It also offered a glimpse of what you might expect from well-motivated and committed people. Attempts to gain people's commitment in order to improve performance must be a long-term and continuous process. Consequently, you would be wise to subdue 'knee-jerk' reactions to short-term people problems. Shorter-term restraint from managers is likely to lead to a longer-term understanding of people's perceptions and the effects of these perceptions on their everyday work. My general advice for managers is as follows:

- The task of management is to ensure that the right people are in the right job with the right competencies at the right time. Your role also includes responsibility for providing a context within which employees can have, and maintain, the right attitude.
- Watch out for any behavioural signs that suggest your people are discontented or frustrated with their job, such as frequently arriving late, taking extended lunchbreaks, looking bored with

their job and so on. Ask your people how things are going –
then listen to their answer and watch out for those telltale non-
verbal signals.

- Continuously assess new information against current and past
  information on employee satisfaction and commitment levels.
  Bear in mind that we all have a bad day every now and again.
  It's best to acknowledge that human beings sometimes act in a
  peculiar way ('there's none as queer as folk') and accept it.
  Nevertheless, watch out for distinct differences in performance
  or behaviour and make a suitable early intervention – even if it
  is only a short chat on-site to check for problems that will
  affect performance. In other words, get to know your people
  well.

- Work hard to improve your competence with techniques that
  help enable high performance – that is, recruiting, selecting,
  inducting, appraising, training, developing, coaching and
  counselling. These skills and techniques are your toolkit –
  leaving them in the toolbox will not get the job done well.
  However, when you employ them consider and accept that
  fluctuations and delays may occur before improvements
  become obvious. When you make an intervention – for
  example, when you decide to counsel or coach someone in
  order to find out what is leading to poor performance – you
  must accept that it is naive, in most cases, to expect immediate
  improvements. Wait a while, then check to see whether small
  improvements occur over a reasonable period of time. If they
  don't, make a further 'skills' intervention from your toolbox.

- Avoid short-term 'quick-fire' interventions, such as shouting at
  an employee in front of their colleagues. Although it may
  provide immediate results, the employee will never forget or
  forgive you for embarrassing them, so the chances of their
  being committed to you and your company in the future are
  very low.

- A balanced style of management and leadership is most often
  the best – that is, firm but fair, decisive and assertive rather
  than aggressive and autocratic, showing a concern for
  production but an equal concern for people and so on.
  Occasionally rereading Chapter 2 may pay dividends.

- If nothing else, you should accept that motivational activities
  relating to control of the work itself, such as worker
  participation, training and development, work rotation, job
  enhancement and so on, are all within your scope as manager.
  You can shape and change the jobs people do; you can
  enhance and enrich jobs; you can give your people more
  responsibility, you can empower them and provide for greater
  achievement in the job. Remember, all Herzberg's motivational factors are in some way under your jurisdiction. The
  general message is clear: management, regardless of level,
  should consider potential impact on employee commitment
  when designing jobs, recruiting, restructuring, communicating

*'I find the harder I work
the more luck I seem to
have.' (Thomas
Jefferson)*

and rewarding employees, when making strategic and project decisions, when conducting appraisals, and when planning and implementing training and development activities.

- Learn from the process of management; do not simply acknowledge it. Managers need to learn from doing and, most importantly, reflecting on the outcomes of their actions. Without reflection – that is, thinking about what you said and did and what the results were – learning cannot take place and you cannot improve. Asking yourself questions about problems, seeking answers to problems and then reflecting on the appropriateness of decisions is the route to improvement. Remember, perfection will always escape you.

- It is well worth remembering that employees are now better educated and more litigious. Moreover, the extent to which they feel an obligation to any one employer is decreasing. Clearly, you must be sensitive to the needs and rights of your people. Most employees reluctantly accept that business risk inherently involves them in personal/job risk. What they seem to find unacceptable is feeling that they are not considered as an integral element of the business. Employees are expected to invest their physical and mental capital, their skills, time, knowledge and dedication to the firm. However, just as managers see their business as a process of risk and return, so do people. From their perspective, a good return for their risk is in the hands of managers. People have commented that being referred to as a 'human resource' often means being treated as an exploitable 'resource', but not necessarily in a 'human' manner. The term has unfortunate connotations that remind people that their status is similar to that of financial and physical resources. However, as mentioned in Chapters 2, 3 and 4, managers and the firm can show recognition for people in almost everything they say and do – your task is to achieve some balance in the eyes of your people.

'If a manager does his or her best, what else is there?' (From a quote by General George S. Patton)

It is now very acceptable to suggest that one of the hallmarks of leading-edge organizations has been the successful adoption and application by their managers of performance measurement. As you now know, the performance management process informs managers about the organizational effectiveness and efficiency of its processes, helps decision-making, and generally helps them manage resources – including people.

The balanced scorecard (BSC) and the EFQM Excellence Model^{TM} are tools that allow you to identify and use a limited number of company performance measures to drive business improvement. Both models have been widely adopted in recent years.

The Balanced Scorecard

Adopting the Balanced Scorecard (Kaplan and Norton, 1996) terminology, Templeton College interviewed board-level executives from 23 leading multinational companies across several industry sectors. They found that 80 per cent of the more successful high-performing companies involved the use of broad 'transformational scorecards'. So what is it all about?

The Balanced Scorecard idea emerged from a sponsored one-year multi-company study by Kaplan and Norton. Their research was motivated by a belief that existing performance measurement approaches relied too heavily on financial measures. Their original ideas about the development of a Balanced Scorecard simply suggest that, whatever the strategic goals of the organization, benefits will occur if many measurement dimensions are monitored rather than just financial measures. The model is built on a few assumptions:

- that you are able to identify things to do, which will lead to important outcomes being achieved
- that, given appropriate feedback, you will identify ways to improve performance
- that most organizations rely on management activity performed by teams as well as by individuals
- that, in any firm, clear communication of goals, priorities and expectations is required to achieve high-level performance.

The Balanced Scorecard approach is often mentioned when company strategy and, in particular, performance management is being considered. Although the process needs to be thought through, agreed and communicated effectively, it is worth remembering that the approach relates and embellishes commonly known performance measurement and management techniques. Consequently, it fits very well with most of this book, particularly with the sections covering the performance management process, performance measures and agreement, using measures to monitor performance, and performance review.

The Balanced Scorecard (see Figure 5.1) provides a structured methodology for translating company objectives into a set (or clusters) of performance measures. By clustering performance measures under four areas – financial, customer, internal business processes, and learning and growth (or innovation) – the company is better able to prioritize resources and, through the monitoring process, shape and reshape direction. The process helps you to see how the different areas of the firm (all requiring excellent performance) are integrated. Operational performance measures that you may use day-to-day are simply a part of one or more of the four BSC strategic clusters.

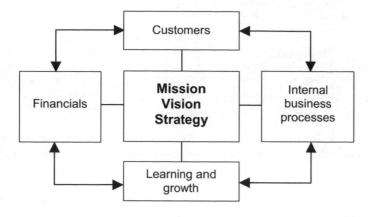

Figure 5.1 *The Balanced Scorecard – strategic objectives*

If you are reading this section and thinking that the Balanced Scorecard is only something of interest to senior management, you would be wrong. The concept must be executed at all levels of the organization. It is suggested that senior managers should instigate and then employ the balanced scorecard approach by first ensuring that they communicate effectively to all managers and employees what a Balanced Scorecard looks like at all levels of the organization. Once this is done, it will be up to all managers and supervisors to make sure that the clearly communicated message is put into practice.

Clusters

It is worth providing some detail on each of the Balanced Scorecard clusters.

Customers – 'How do our customers see us?' and 'What must we excel at?'

This measure focuses on how the company is seen by its customers or clients. Of course, most firms know the importance of ensuring that customers perceive that they are receiving good products and service. However, the balanced scorecard forces managers to identify and maintain those measurable characteristics that are valued by customers. Typically, customers evaluate a firm's performance based on four areas: time, quality, product and/or service, and cost. A firm might therefore use KPIs such as delivery on time, defect rates, number of returns, warranty claims, or ratings obtained through customer satisfaction surveys. Whatever the measurement, the idea is that the manager tries to see the product and/or service from the customer's perspective – through their eyes.

Financials – 'What profit do we need?' and 'How can we ensure our costs are controlled?'

Financial measures have traditionally been the main focus of performance measurement. Consequently, the Balanced Scorecard model allows the firm to focus on how it is viewed by its shareholders. Measurements used would include return on investment, return and capital employed, profit before tax and so on. However, high-level financial targets have been criticized for their historic or backward-looking focus and the possible disconnect between company performance and, for example, site operational performance. Clearly, related 'operational' performance measures must include budget-holder spending, control of costs, cash forecasting and so on. Generally, it makes sense for managers to employ good day-to-day financial housekeeping – they should manage their budgets efficiently and effectively. This might be best achieved by managers and supervisors making sure that they understand how their contribution at operational levels makes (or breaks) the company's overall financial performance – the bottom line. You may wish to seek training in 'money management techniques'. It is not necessary for you to become an accountant, only to know how money works, how to control spending, and how you and your team(s) play their part. Simply, knowing how money is used in your company is a prerequisite to controlling it.

Internal business processes – 'What must we excel at?' and 'What internal processes add value?'

This part of the balanced scorecard attempts to ensure that internal processes add value to satisfying customer needs that in turn leads to financial success. To meet organizational objectives and customer expectations, organizations must identify, monitor and improve the important business processes at which they must excel. Such processes typically include cycle time, quality performance, productivity, delivery on time, and pre-contract and post-contract service. Although not always explicitly stated by companies using the BSC model, people must excel in every way. You should identify core competencies that lead to high business performance and use specific indicators for measuring people success, such as those described in Chapter 4.

Learning and growth (innovation) – 'What do we need to do to grow the business?' and 'Can we continue to improve?'

The company cannot survive and grow on the basis of internal processes and targets related to current products/service/operations alone – it needs to innovate. Standing still means being left behind as the industry progressively improves. An innovative, or learning, dimension helps the company remain forward-focused by encouraging continuous improvements and innovations. Measures might include the number of improvements to service, the time taken to introduce technological improvements, number of investment/project appraisal applications, improvements required in the quality of information available and so on. This BSC perspective also looks at employees' abilities; a firm cannot learn on its own – only people learn. It is people, not machines, who have the ability to generate new ideas. As a result, balanced scorecards also include measures of employee satisfaction, employee turnover and the number of innovative suggestions.

Measurement and balance

Measurement is clearly crucial, and identifying several areas for measurement, in addition to the financial area, is admirable and more likely to capture the reality of the organization's context – including various stakeholders. Balance suggests the steadiness that results when all the firm's priorities are properly adjusted to each other and where no one priority is outweighing others. We hear of balanced diets being healthy, balanced wheels being safer, balanced budgets helping to sustain growth, people being well-balanced and so on; being balanced leads to health (organizational, mental or physical) which leads to efficiency and effectiveness. Adopting a balanced number of areas to measure and review – for example, to include measures related to the firm's contribution to society or to measure employee satisfaction and their commitment to the firm – may run counter to the traditional view that the company should only be interested in maximizing profit. Nonetheless, the incentive for managers and the organization's principal owners is clear. Balanced scorecards help you understand what really drives success in your firm and within your immediate working environment.

'One accurate measurement is worth more than a thousand expert opinions.' (Admiral Grace Hopper)

If you concentrate on critical indicators of both current and future performance, trends can emerge that help you focus on areas requiring improvement. Of course, the need for motivated and committed employees is critical to ensuring business improvement – regardless of the indicator/measure chosen. However, the application of a balanced scorecard methodology should lead to greater employee satisfaction. Higher levels of job satisfaction should lead to improved employee self-esteem and increased levels of commitment, and, as discussed, employee commitment results in individual and organizational performance improvements – what might be called a 'virtuous circle of improvement'.

Implementing a Balanced Scorecard methodology

Steps required to implement a Balanced Scorecard performance management strategy would include the following:

1   Agree the firm's vision, mission and strategy.

2 Establish performance measures in line with objectives and goals and set within each of the four clusters.
3 Collect data.
4 Analyse data.
5 Manage performance by using the analysed data so that positive action results in change.
6 Let the process and manager ability evolve with experience.

The EFQM Excellence Model™

I do not intend to explain in detail the intricacies of the European Foundation for Quality Management (EFQM) Excellence Model™, but simply to refer readers to the model and add explanation as to links between key aspects of this book.

The EFQM was formed in 1988 by the presidents of 14 European companies when they realized that global competition was threatening Europe's market position. Its mission was to promote and assist European managers to understand and apply total quality principles. The model has been widely used by organizations worldwide, not least those in the construction industry.

The intention of the EFQM Excellence Model™ is to provide a framework that organizations wishing to define and work towards organizational excellence can adopt as part of their decision-making framework. How does it work? The model assumes that managers require excellence and that excellence can be gained by considering the five 'enabling' criteria – leadership, people, policy and strategy, partnerships and resources, and processes – and the four 'results' criteria – performance, customers, people, and society (see Figure 5.2). Current performance on all these aspects is evaluated as a score across the nine criteria by the use of standard questions – for example, 'Are processes systematically designed and managed?'. Scores on all questions are used for either internal self-assessment as a benchmark for improvement or, with the assistance of an internal or external trained specialist, can be assessed against a universal scoring and weighting system where no adjustments are made for the size of organization or type of industry. The use of external specialists is often associated with a company's wish to win a European Quality Award.

The scoring system of the model suggests that 90 points should be allocated to people results, 60 points to social results and 200 points to customer results. However, from the perspective of improving the manager–employee relationship, this weighting seems inappropriate because, although monitoring of all key performance results are important, distinguishing customers as 'more important' and people as 'less important' might be damaging. It inadvertently puts barriers in the way of potentially highly committed high-performing employees. Perhaps equal weighting in terms of key result areas would be more appropriate – similar to the Balanced Scorecard idea.

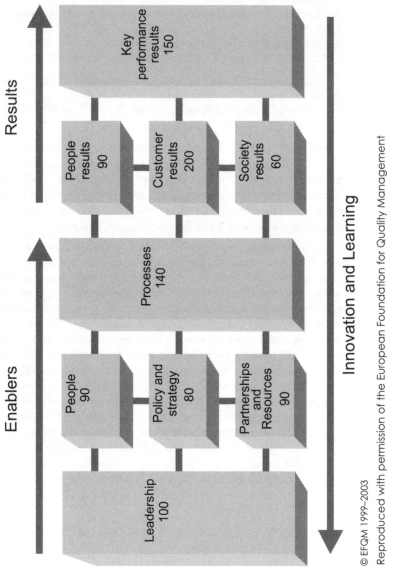

© EFQM 1999–2003

Reproduced with permission of the European Foundation for Quality Management

Figure 5.2 *The EFQM Excellence Model*™

The whole EFQM system is related to improving overall performance. The questions used to assess the nine areas of the model are clearly related to the kind of performance measures discussed in Chapter 4. Improvements can be achieved by using techniques and processes such as improving communication, recruitment, selection, coaching and so on as discussed in Chapter 3. Also contained within the EFQM Excellence Model™, are several aspects that might be directly influenced by issues discussed in Chapter 2, such as leadership, management behaviour and employee motivation. For example, leadership in the model is described as 'How leaders develop and facilitate the achievement of the mission and vision, develop values required for long-term success and implement these via appropriate actions and behaviours' – does this sound familiar?

The EFQM Excellence Model™ urges active leader involvement and talks of appropriate leader behaviour. Unfortunately, it is not clear as to what would be regarded as appropriate, although one of the EFQM sub-criteria does suggest that leaders need to motivate, support and recognize the organization's people.

The model goes out of its way to indicate the need to monitor both qualitative and quantitative measures. This is similar to the approach to performance management given in Chapter 4. Questions about people, motivational needs and commitment as 'enablers' might form an integral part of the leadership 'enablers' section of the model. The same issues could also be used as part of the people 'results' element within project and business planning review processes, performance review/appraisal processes, training and development plans and competency frameworks as discussed in Chapter 4.

The manager's role in EFQM and BSC modelling

Your role is important because the benefits sought from adopting and using EFQM or BSC modelling is solely dependent on the changes and decisions you make and in the work done by people working in your company. Clearly, the results provide a benchmark by which you might strive through your decisions, actions and behaviour to improve your company's performance.

Continuous improvement can only be gained through learning. Fortunately, the importance of learning runs through the EFQM and the BSC models. Both suggest the need to review results as the means to continuous learning. The need for innovation and learning has also been an ongoing theme throughout all the chapters of this book, so I can't resist saying a little more about learning at the organizational level.

The learning company

Chapter 1 introduced the need for the development of skills and knowledge. The development, sharing and application of knowledge is possibly the number one key driver or utility of a high-performance company. Of course, how knowledge is developed, encouraged, shared and used relies on management skill, especially the ability to create a working environment where the process of transference from brain to valued performance outcomes can occur.

You may have heard of a notion called the learning company/organization. The learning organization is a visionary concept describing the need for individuals, groups or project teams, parts of the organization or the whole firm to learn. Without learning there can be little or no progress, improvement, development or competitive advantage.

Bernard Sullivan, as general manager of Rover in 1996, stated that 'for Rover the learning organisation was really the unlearning organisation'. He states that 'the ultimate challenge is to do things differently ... systems by themselves will not enable change, but marginal changes in the attitudes of people sometimes bring leaps forward.' (cited in Overell, 1996, p. 14). This is my experience exactly – what about yours?

Without encouragement, learning cannot take place and will not form an element of the organization's culture – 'the way we do things around here'.

I suggest that, although managers may understand the effect of employee attitudes on job performance, they are less knowledgeable about its cause. So, try to provide for yourself a steady flow of information that you can analyse, reflect upon and use. Without it, learning will be limited and performance sub-optimized. From my experience of the application of good, if not best, practice, I believe that the explanations, descriptions, techniques and processes offered in this book should assist.

Let's end with a few upbeat answers to the following question: How can a manager encourage a learning environment?

- The use of knowledge is today's new economic resource, so encourage its use.
- Be clear about your objectives and communicate them effectively.
- Remember, people will perform well if you give consideration to what motivates them and act on it – it is the means to secure improvements in employee commitment.
- Take part in training or design – develop and deliver a learning event.
- Assist development – think up ideas to develop people.
- Think about the needs of people in relation to company objectives.

'Be nice to people on your way up because you meet them on your way down.' (Jimmy Durante)

- Identify the gap between current and future skills, knowledge and level of commitment – put forward plans to 'close the gap'.
- When possible, support people's education. Ask them how their further or higher education is going and how they might try a few of the ideas out in the workplace. It may be all academic but, after all, that's where most of the concepts and techniques that you currently use on a day-to-day basis originated.
- Work on training plans, or at least offer your input as to what your people need in order to improve performance.
- Use project work to stimulate new ideas, improve teamwork and overall development.
- Seek the involvement of the team.
- Ask members of your team to take the role of chairperson on a rotating basis.
- Devolve responsibility.
- Delegate when it is appropriate to do so, and especially when the individual can cope and achieve a promising outcome.
- Provide coaching.
- Push for people to self-develop – assist their self-development plans.
- Think about your own and other people's professional and career development.
- Could you be a mentor to a new recruit?
- How about secondments? Would they help broaden your people's outlook and see new ideas or cross-functional improvements?
- Work to make people's jobs more interesting and rewarding. Think about job design, job enrichment, project work, teamworking, empowerment schemes and programmes.
- Promote suggestion and/or innovation schemes.
- Use the appraisal process as a developmental tool. Perhaps ask your staff to appraise your performance – you never know, someone might be brave enough to respond!
- If one of your staff shows stress and their work behaviour falters, try some friendly counselling but be sure to know in what circumstances you need to consult professionals.
- Show respect for people and treat them with consideration while focusing on the task at hand. Make sure that your management style reflects leadership qualities – get some overall balance between task and people/process concerns!

If you adopt the approaches and processes highlighted in this book and develop your people management skills – expect performance to improve. Remember, however, that the development of appropriate and well-honed people management skills will take time – employees may initially be suspicious. Consequently, desired changes will not occur overnight and evidence as to success may be elusive – at least in the short term.

If you have managed to read this entire book, you now know how difficult your job is, so I will end with a prayer and wish you good luck.

A manager's prayer

Dear Lord, help me to become the kind of manager my staff and my boss would like me to be – however impossible this sounds.

Give me the mysterious something that David Cooper talks about which will enable me at all times to explain policies, rules, regulations, objectives, targets and procedures to my people, even when they have never been explained before.

Help me to train, develop, coach and counsel the uninterested without losing my patience.

Give me that love of my fellow man which passeth all understanding, so that I may lead the obstinate poor performing worker into the path of righteousness by my own example and my soft persuading remonstrance, instead of busting them on the nose and getting myself sacked.

I do not want to be a saint; some of my people are and they can be so hard to live with.

Instil into my inner being tranquillity and peace of mind, that no longer will I wake up stressed from my restless sleep in the middle of the night, crying out with newly found open questions, 'What has the boss got that I haven't got, and how did he get it?'

Teach me to smile if it kills me.

Make me a better leader of people by helping develop larger and greater qualities of understanding, tolerance, recognition, sympathy, wisdom, mind-reading and second sight.

And when, dear Lord, thou has helped me to achieve the high performance my management has prescribed for me and for my people, and when I have become the paragon of all management and leadership virtues in this mortal world – dear Lord, move over!

References and Further Reading

Bennis, W.G. (1990), 'Managing the Dream: Leadership in the 21st Century', *Training: The Magazine of Human Resource Development, 27*(5), pp. 44–6.

See also Bennis (2000) in which Bennis reflects on his original ideas.

Bennis, W.G. (2000), *Managing the Dream: Reflections on Leadership and Change*, Boulder, CO: Perseus Books.

CBI (1976), *Priorities for In-Company Communication*, Confederation of British Industry Report prepared by M. Brandon and M. Arnott, London: CBI.

CBI (1981), *Workplace Industrial Relations Survey*, Confederation of British Industry Second Report, London: CBI.

See also CBI (1976).

CITB (2003), Abstract of *Investors in People – CITB – Construction Skills Information* at: <www.constructingexcellence.org.uk/resourcecentre/publications>. Search the site A–Z for Investors in People and then select CITB Construction Skills Information.

Couger, J.D. and Zawacki, R.A. (1980), *Motivating and Managing Computer Personnel: The 1966 Study,* New York: Wiley & Sons.

Department of Trade and Industry (2002), *Construction Statistics Annual:* 2002 Edition, London: The Stationery Office.

European Foundation for Quality Management (EFQM) 1999 – 2003, *The EFQM Excellence Model^{TM}.*

See website and contact details in the Useful Addresses section.

Egan, Sir John (1998), *Rethinking Construction: Report from the Construction Task Force*, London: Department of the Environment, Transport and Regions.

For a download copy see the DTI website: www.dti.gov.uk/construction/rethink/report/index.htm

Or, following registration, download a copy from the Constructing Excellence website: www.constructingexcellence.org.uk

Grim, C. (2001), 'The Changing Environment in the Construction Industry – Guidelines for Survival and Growth', paper presented at the BER Building and Construction Conference, Rosebank, Johannesburg.

Health and Safety Executive (2002), 'Revitalising Health and Safety within HSE', *Health and Safety Executive Annual Report 2001.2002.*

HSE contact details are listed in the Useful Addresses section of this book.

Herzberg, F. (1966), *Work and the Nature of Man*, New York: Staples Press.

Institute of Directors (1991), *Communications at Work: The Challenge and the Response. A Survey of Communication within Britain's Medium-sized and Larger Companies*, London: Institute of Directors (IoD) and Bolton Dickinson Associates.

Kaplan, R.S. and Norton, D.P. (1993), Putting the Balanced Scorecard to Work, *Harvard Business Review*, September–October, pp.134–47.

Kaplan, R.S. and Norton, D.P. (1996), *The Balanced Scorecard,* Boston, MA: Harvard Business School Press.

Kotter, J.P. (1990a), *Force for Change: How Leadership Differs from Management*, New York: The Free Press.

Kotter, J.P. (1990b), 'What Leaders Really Do'*, Harvard Business Review, 1* (47), pp. 59–67.

Kovach, K.A. (1987), 'What Motivates Employees? Workers and Managers Give Different Answers', *Business Horizons*, (30), pp. 58–65.

Labour Force Survey (2002). See National Statistics website: <www.statistics.gov.uk>

Lundy, J.L. (1957), *Effective Industrial Management*, London: Macmillan.

McGregor, D. (1960), *The Human Side of Enterprise*, New York: McGraw-Hill.

McGregor, D. (1966), *Leadership and Motivation*, Cambridge, MA: MIT Press.

Maslow, A.H. (1943), 'A Theory of Human Motivation', *Psychological Review*, July, pp. 370–96.

Maslow, A.H. (1954), *Motivation and Personality*, New York: Harper.

Mole, T. (2003), 'Mind Your Manners'*, Proceedings of the CIB W89 Symposium, International Conference on Building Education and Research (BEAR),* School of Construction and Property Management, Built and Human Environment Research Institute, University of Salford, April, pp. 286–99.

Murray, H.A. (1938), *Exploration in Personality*, New York: John Wiley and Sons.

Overell, S. (1996), *'*Learning to Unlearn for a Flexible Future'*, People Management,* 2(1).

Pedler, M.J., Burgoyne, J.G. and Boydell, T. (1995) *The Learning Company: A Strategy for Substantial Development*, New York: McGraw-Hill.

Respect for People Working Group (2002), *Reaching the Standard*, London: Rethinking Construction Ltd.

See also: www.constructingexcellence.org.uk

Respect for People toolkits are available from Constructing Excellence, 25 Buckingham Palace Road, London SW1W 0PP.

Respect for People Working Group (2003a), *Respect for People: A Framework for Action*, London: Rethinking Construction Ltd.

This report is also available at: www.constructingexcellence.org/rc/respect/publications/reports.asp

Respect for People Working Group (2003b), *A Commitment to People – Our Biggest Asset: A Report from the Movement for Innovation's Working Group on Respect for People*, London: Rethinking Construction Ltd.

A copy of this report is available from: <www.constructingexcellence.org/rc/respect/publications/reports>. Refer to document URN 00/1693.

The Strategic Forum for Construction (2002), *Rethinking Construction – Accelerating Change*, London: Department of Trade and Industry.

A copy of the report is available via the DTI website: www.dti.gov.uk/construction

Or, following registration, download a copy from the Constructing Excellence website: www.constructingexcellence.org.uk

Taylor, J.W. (1962), *How to Select and Develop Leaders*, New York: McGraw-Hill.

Tichy, N.M. and Devanna, M.A. (1986), *Transformational Leadership*, New York: Wiley.

The British Quality Foundation
32–34 Great Peter Street
London SW1P 2QX
Tel: 020 7654 5000
Website: www.quality-foundation.co.uk

Building Software Ltd
Swallow Court
Devonshire Gate
Sampford Peverell
Tiverton
Devon EX16 7EJ
Tel: 01884 841884
Fax: 01884 849114
e-mail: info@buildsoft.co.uk
Website: www.buildsoft.co.uk/clubs
(For details of benchmarking clubs)

Constructing Excellence
25 Buckingham Palace Road
Victoria
London SW1W 0PP
Tel: 020 7592 1100
Fax: 020 7592 1101
Helpdesk: 0845 605 5556
e-mail: helpdesk@constructingexcellence.org.uk
Website: www.constructingexcellence.org.uk
(For the Construction Best Practice Programme and Constructing Excellence Clubs)

Construction Industry Training Board (CITB)
Head Office:
Bircham Newton
King's Lynn
Norfolk PE31 6RH
Tel: 01485 577577
Fax: 01485 577793
e-mail: information.centre@citb.co.uk
Website: www.citb.org.uk
(Contact the head office or consult the website for the address of the nearest local office)

European Foundation for Quality Management (EFQM)
P.O. Box 6386
NL-5600HJ Eindhoven
The Netherlands
Tel: +32 2 775 3511
Fax: +32 2 775 3535
e-mail: info@efqm.org
Website: www.efqm.org
(For information on the EFQM Excellence Model™)

Gower Publishing Ltd
Gower House
Croft Road
Aldershot
Hampshire GU11 3HR
Tel: 01252 331551
Fax: 01252 344405
e-mail: info@gowerpub.com
Website: www.gowerpub.com

Health and Safety Executive
For regional offices:
Tel: 08701 545500
Fax: 02920 859260
e-mail: hseinformationservices@natbrit.com
Website: www.hse.gov.uk

International Organization for Standardization (ISO)
Website: www.iso.org

Investors in People
7-10 Chandos Street
London W1G 9DQ
Tel: 020 7467 1900
Fax: 020 7636 2386
e-mail: information@iipuk.co.uk
Website: www.investorsinpeople.co.uk

The National Business Link (Benchmark Index) Service
Website: www.benchmarkindex.com

Office for National Statistics
Customer Contact Centre
Room 1.015
Office for National Statistics
Cardiff Road
Newport
Wales NP10 8XG
Tel: 0845 601 3034
Fax: 01633 652747
e-mail: info@statistics.gov.uk
Website: www.statistics.gov.uk

absence monitoring   111–13
accelerating change (in construction)   4, 85, 134
appraising   118–25
   360° approach *see also* feedback   126
   and feedback   64, 69–71, 88, 126
   process   141, 155
assessment centres   79

Balanced Scorecard (BSC)   147–51
benchmarking   108–10, 114–17
budgetary control   110, 149

change in construction   2, 142, 144
   and government initiatives   3, 85
CITB   11, 129, 134–5
coaching   91–3
commitment   17, 24, 30–32
communication   57–8
   and assertive behaviour   61
   asking questions   69
   formal   58
   giving and receiving feedback   88
   grapevine   68
   informal   68–9
   interpersonal   60, 93, 140
   mission statements   54–5
   non-verbal   77, 97
   presentations   89–90
   and time management   9, 61, 64, 66
   written   67
competence and competencies   9–17, 41, 82, 93
competition   2, 72, 151
conflict   104, 139–41
construction industry: context   2
Construction Industry Training Board *see* CITB
content theories of motivation   34
contextual challenges   2–18
   health and safety   5–7
   knowledge economy   17
costs   13, 40, 99, 105, 107–10, 115–16
culture   29, 32, 133–4

decisions   13–14, 24, 32, 146
delegation   91
developing people   92, 127–34

education   45, 75, 100, 127–33, 155
efficiency   30, 38, 110, 150
EFQM   151–3
employee – manager/leader relations   7
employee
   needs   34–6
   recognition   35, 46–9
   and trust   30, 56, 97
empowerment   32, 40, 114
extrinsic motivation   37

feedback   29, 38
   see also appraising and feedback
   360°   126
   giving and receiving   88, 91
   see also appraising and feedback
flexibility   43, 84
followership   23, 29–33

goals   21, 27, 105
government initiatives for change   3–5

health and safety (in construction)   5–7
hierarchy of needs   35–6
human resource management and strategy   54

inducting (managing the first day)   80
injuries in construction   6
intrinsic motivation   37
Investors in People (IiP)   111, 134–5
involvement and participation   32, 53, 145

job content   40
job description   73, 76
job enlargement   40
job enrichment   40–41
job rotation   39
job satisfaction and commitment   36–41
job specification   74, 137

key performance indicators (KPIs) 105, 107–12,
                                              116
knowledge economy (in the construction
   industry)   17

leadership   2, 14, 20–30

characteristics of leaders 20
links with the Balanced Scorecard 145–7
transformational 27–8, 30
learning contracts 95, 106, 127–8
learning organization 154

management development 127, 129–34
management style
   see also Theory 'X' and 'Y' 24–5
manager as
   appraiser 118–25
   coach 91–3
   counsellor 95–7
   mentor 93–5
   trainer 87–90
managers and leaders 20
managing stress 61–4
mentoring 93
mission statements 54–5
motivation 32–50
   and employee achievement 35–8
   and employee satisfaction 36–7
   extrinsic 37
   growth factors 37
   hierarchy of needs 35–6
   hygiene factors 38, 99
   intrinsic 37
   money as a motivator 33, 42, 48
   natural recognition 48–9
   need theories 34–6
   recognition 46–9
   worker and manager perspectives 46–7

National Vocational Qualifications
   (NVQs) 10, 45
needs 35

operational performance measures 107, 147, 149
organizational culture 129

participation 145
pay 11, 41–2
perception 8, 126
performance
   and agreements 105–6
   and appraisals/reviews 118–25
   behavioural performance 117–18
   contracts 105
   different standards 121
   future strategies 144
   gaps 4, 116
   halo effect 121
   measures 43, 107–10
   and personnel policies/procedures 56

process 104–5
PRP schemes 42–4
related pay 42
reports/reporting results 107
setting objectives 95, 105
SMART objective setting 106–7
timing and recency 104, 122, 132
performance indicators (KPIs) 107–12
performance management 7
performance measures 107–10
performance results 21, 30, 60, 85–6, 116
person specification 75, 137
personal development 46, 106, 120, 133–4
profit and profitability 13, 86, 109–10, 149
psychometric tests 78

qualities of leaders 28–30
qualities of managers 21, 28

recognition 46–9
recruiting and selecting people 72–80
Respect for People –
   Framework for Action 4, 7
   Reaching the Standard 5
retaining good people 52, 98–101
Rethinking Construction 4, 72, 135
rewards and incentives 42–9

selection tests 78
self-development 127
self-esteem 36, 40–41, 150
shareholders 144, 149
stakeholders 102, 144
strategy and strategic plans 53
stress (how to manage it) 64

targets 3–5, 44, 105
teams 82
   briefings 85–6
   building teams 82–3
   and commitment 82, 84, 87
   and development 83
   and leadership 84–5
Theory 'X' 26
Theory 'Y' 27
time management 9, 61, 64, 66
total quality principles 151
training and development 100, 127–31
transformational leadership 27–8

values 28, 55, 58, 139–40

written communication 67–8

Further Titles in the Leading Construction Series

Project Management in Construction
Dennis Lock
Hardback   208 pages   244 x 172 mm   0 566 08612 3

Quality Management in Construction
Third Edition
Brian Thorpe and Peter Sumner
Hardback   240 pages   244 x 172 mm   0 566 08614 X

Improving People Performance in Construction
David Cooper
Hardback   184 pages   244 x 172 mm   0 566 08617 4

Winning New Business in Construction
Terry Gillen
Hardback   c. 130 pages   244 x 172 mm   0 566 08615 8

For more details of these books or new titles in the series visit www.gowerpub.com or contact our sales department:

Sales Department, Gower Publishing Limited, Gower House, Croft Road, Aldershot, Hants, GU11 3HR, UK. Tel: +44 (0)1252 331551; e-mail: info@gowerpub.com